SLOW + SACRED

Waking To The Whispers Of God In Every Season

Nina Landis

The moment I began to read 'Slow + Sacred' I thought, "This is going to be a devotional classic." These are words that spring from a heart that has hungered and found and still hungered for more – of God. More than lines with rhymes on a page – it's poetry and passion drawn deep from the wells of God's singer of songs Nina Landis. It's a primordial call of the wild to the ancient paths of the pursuit and the findings of God in the ordinary rhythms of life. It's a rediscovery of the artesian well that will deliver us from the drying, dying treadmill of ministry drivenness, the causeway of the crash. Read, return, and find refreshment for your soul.

Lou Engle, President of Lou Engle Ministries, Founder of The Call

Nina had me at "With this book I declare war on that liar." Of course, she does, and of course, this book will. Nina is the only creative I know that beats a war drum while kissing God's cheek. She shifts atmospheres with her words, whether sung, spoken, or written. This book is for the rowdy and the weary, the loud and the quiet. It's for the body of Christ, afflicted but not crushed, struck down but not destroyed. Let the words in this book take you closer to The One who is The Word, fights for you, and loves you deeply in and out of every season.

Alisa Keeton, founder of Revelation Wellness,
best-selling author The Body Revelation

Nina is everyone's favorite person, whether you spend a half day or two decades with her. Her love for life, family, and friends is only eclipsed by her humble and intimate walk with Jesus. 'Slow + Sacred' had me from the invitation… "dreaming of a day when we will all together wake to the fullness of this miraculous and profound gift… GOD WITH US." Page after page and contemplation after contemplation probe all the aesthetics of our wondrous and complicated lives – seasons, rhythms, colors, sounds, stillness, silence, shadow, and light. All and everything point to a sacred truth. In Jesus, God has drawn so much closer to you than you know! In Christ, God has a tender acquaintance with you. He knows every season, every thought, every moment, every emotion, and every bodily joy and problem. He is intimately familiar with you, not from writing a manual on human design but from joining Himself to you in the nitty gritty of our weak and beautiful lives – forever! Nina reminds us in the most creative and subtle ways that Jesus has made all space and season grace-filled and that it is OK to love Him there.

Allen Hood, Director of Excellencies of Christ Ministries

'Slow + Sacred' is a masterful work, interweaving rhythmic wisdom and exquisite writing. Nina's words resonate deeply, urging us to abandon the ceaseless pulls of modern life and embrace the serene rhythms of being the beloved of God. Through her eloquent expression, she poignantly reminds us of life's true essence and significance. This book is a heartfelt invitation to rediscover our sacred purpose amidst the noise, making it a profoundly enriching read.

Anna Asbury, Art Creator & Writer

Right now, as I look at the breakdown, pain, and need in my generation (with an awareness of the younger ones watching and taking cues as to what to either follow or refuse) I believe there is a needed antidote beyond the pressure of: bigger, shinier, and louder, that is answered with what is: deeper, truer, and quieter. My friend Nina is a generous, and lived soul, whose presence makes you feel loved, and worth being known, who also inspires you to love with a witness that could only come from Love Himself. She is not scared of the hard questions. She has stories and real imprints of when Divinity and humanity meet. She is a treasure chest of experiences in meeting God in sorrow, joy, confusion, with a broken heart, with abundance, in loss, and in everyday simplicity. More now, than ever, I believe we need stories of mothers and fathers to companion us in our journey of faith, over "how to" guides or quick fixes. Nina's stories are a well-worn path, like the tear-stained book of Psalms you return to. These words provide deep comfort and light. She is a friend I deeply love. Her words drip from her own path and story where Jesus as Emmanuel has met her and will be a helpful friend for anyone wanting to deepen their authentic love and devotion to Christ in a truer and quieter way.

Cassie Campbell, Friend, Musician, Teacher, Fellow Disciple

This book seems a lifetime in the making. I've been waiting for something like this. A book that actually leads and shepherds me into deeper intimacy, healing and union with God. Like an old friend, Nina so effortlessly and transparently shepherds me to dropping my masks and walls so that I can receive from the Lord. What makes this offering different is that it is not defined by flowery truth that denies the wrestle and struggle of real life. The truths presented here have the essence of authentic and real battles fought and won. The full scope of life with God is present. All the joy, hope, crushing, mystery, and bliss of real life with Jesus is here. A future classic! I'm sure of it!

Chris Burns, Musician, Author of *Pioneers of His Presence* and *The Priesthood*

For years I've relished Nina's authentically deep posts that would pop up as an oasis in the midst of the dry dessert of social media's surface clutter. I thought if she ever wrote a book anything like the simple yet profound prophetic songs she sings, I'd love to read it! Finally, this worship leader pours into the pages of a book the unique sounds of a heart that come from each season of the soul— helping, those who are willing to follow, find a well-traveled path into the heart of a Father who adores us through it all.

Elizabeth Enlow, Co-Founder of Restore7, Author of *Rainbow God, God in Every Season, RISE: A Handbook for Reformers on the Seven Mountains,* and *Students on the RISE*

For a FREE downloadable Bible resource
companion to Slow + Sacred visit:

www.slowandsacred.com

To the ones who don't know they are seen…

CONTENTS

FOREWORD

The year was 2011 and I felt as though I had just stepped off a fast-moving, never-ending carousel. The word dizzy comes to mind, but it falls short to adequately describe the reeling that took place once my husband and I had stepped off this merry-go-round of sorts. We had responded to an invitation to serve a friend's ministry, and with eyes aglow and hearts full of wonder, hope and expectation, our answer was a resounding yes. Yet, little did we know, what awaited us. In the early years of our marriage, during the span of time between 2008-2011, we gave ourselves for a cause that many just like us, wide-eyed in wonder, would dream of. We traveled from our homeland of Australia to live for a time in the United States and were grateful to travel to other countries around the world in this venture of serving Jesus in ministry. We left everything behind to lay our lives down for the gospel and I would not change that for a moment. It was the invitation of adventure and servitude that our hearts had longed for, and in many ways, it was a fulfillment of those dreams. However, what we did not anticipate, is that this time would be as a training ground for us – a living manual of 'how to burn yourself to the ground.' Or rather, "all the ways you should *not* do ministry."

In the months and years that followed, we would find that our time was no longer our own as we answered to the calendar demands of our friend's ministry, and perpetual sleepless nights catching red eye flights, followed by continuous stretching days of ministry became the norm. No sleep. No rest. No solitude. No time to be found to look into the eyes of Jesus. No moments of repose to open a page in my Bible. We were the epitome of the phrase, 'burning the candle at both ends." My husband, Nate and I, naively made the assumption, *"this is what ministry is, this is the sacrifice required of us, our 'cross' to bare."* I'm grateful we eventually emerged from those subtle delusions when we did, for had we not, I doubt I would be writing these words to you here, today. I imagine, we likely would have done away with our calling to ministry before it ever properly began. I've watched this effect, grievously take place in the lives of others feeling this same burden to the call, only to observe them collapse more quickly than they began. For there has been a widespread lie that has infiltrated the hearts of many, regardless of what your ministry looks like- whether traditional ministry, working in business or the holy call of raising children, many have believed, fast and furious, is the pace of the call. I came to this realization when I miraculously found the time to open my Bible one day and read of Jesus retreating to the mountain to be with the Father – scripture tells us, "as was his habit." (Luke 22:39) Though the demands of His ministry were far greater than ours ever were, His need to minister to the heart of His Father, trumped every other requirement.

My dear friend and author, Nina Landis, is tackling these lies of rush and hurry within the beautiful confines of infallible truth and intimacy. Though I have known her but a short time, hers is a friendship that echoes beyond time, she is the kind of friend you feel you have always known. I muse that the reason for this is because her life, her character, her demeanor, even her family and home, are fused with the very fragrance of another familiar friend of mine, Jesus. There are those in ministry, and then there are those – in ministry to the King. Nina is of the latter camp. Her life inspires and convicts mine in ways that few can. There is a remarkable beauty about her life that draws you in, and I recognize the familiarity of what that glow is – it is indeed, intimacy with Jesus. Nina's words in the pages to follow, are written from the depths of a heart

that beats as one with His. I can tell you, to find someone
who lives this true calling – that our first ministry is to serve
His heart above all else – is a rarity in our day. She lives to
minister to her King. Which is why, "Slow + Sacred" is such
a gift to the Body of Christ, not only in this hour, but I believe
in the days to come. This book, birthed from the very core
of her time with Jesus, holds a treasury of invitations into
intimacy. Laced with poetic wisdom and stunning artistry,
it echoes our first and true calling to come up higher above
the noise of hustle and learn the rhythms of His grace. There,
in the secret place, creativity, answers and solutions are
elicited in ways that can never be obtained in our natural
understanding – Nina exemplifies this dance of bending to his
ear, and creating from His whispers, so exquisitely within her
writings and art.

"Slow + Sacred", is the manual of ministering to the heart of
the Father that my husband and I needed in our early days.
What we learned through pain and disillusionment, I implore
you, follow Nina's call to discover the slow and the sacred –
through the doorway of the Cross – it's where your complete
victory lies.

"Listen, my radiant one – if you ever lose sight of me, just
follow in my footsteps where I lead my lovers. Come with
your burdens and cares. Come to the place near the sanctuary
of my shepherds. My dearest one, let me tell you how I see
you – you are so thrilling to me. To gaze upon you is like
looking at one of Pharaoh's finest horses – a strong, regal
steed pulling his royal chariot. Your tender cheeks are
beautiful – your earrings and gem-laden necklaces set them
ablaze. We will enhance your beauty, with golden ornaments
studded with silver." Song of Songs 1:8-11 TPT

-     Christy Johnston
      Author of *The Deborah Mantle* and *The Esther Mantle*.

AN INVITATION...

I've been aching for you, friend. Carrying a longing in my soul for you to know this great mystery that I am still discovering… that I have only scratched the surface of.

I have been holding you in my thoughts… whispering of you in my prayers… dreaming of a day when we will all together wake to the fullness of this miraculous and profound gift…

GOD

WITH

US.

I know the tyrant of our souls has whispered to you the same lies he's whispered to me. I know the wrestle that comes in the dark hours of the night, when you see a world around you seemingly thriving, and the ache in your own soul is like an internal bleed. No one sees it, but you know it's there. You know your own boot strapping will only last so long before every system fails.

I know that clanging sound on the inside that creeps in and suddenly shoots off with the accusations that you aren't good, you're doing it wrong, and you aren't doing enough. That splintered whisper that says you're alone in

21

your struggle, there's no common language between God and man, and the way you relate to God is different than the way others relate to Him.

Or maybe it sounds like, "You'll never feel close to Him or truly known. He's frustrated with you… impatient with you… weary of you. He's hiding from you and making it difficult to be found, and somehow you better figure out how to climb that spiritual ladder to some mystical place of enlightenment because only THERE will you FINALLY have arrived at a true sense of oneness with God. After all, true fellowship with God must be reserved for a select few and you just aren't one of the lucky ones."

Does any of that sound familiar? Oh, Friend, you are not alone.

I too, have been on a long journey of pain, loss, disappointment, and loneliness. On the way, I have stumbled clumsily and heavy with burden into the miracle of Immanuel. The God who is WITH me.

I have also discovered that there is a very real enemy desperately trying to keep us separated from the SIMPLICITY of devotion to Christ.

With this book, I declare war on that liar.

My deep ache and desire is that you would discover, like I have discovered, that the most beautiful, kind, patient, and perfectly loving God is…

Right here.

Right now.

He isn't hiding from you. He isn't accusing you or disappointed in your humanity and wrestle. No, Friend… He is PRESENT. He is acquainted with you in ALL of your ways.

He's not angry.

He's LONGING.

Leaning into your subtle glance with delight and passion and deep desire to be WITH YOU. Not in the super-spiritual ways that we brush up against on a Sunday morning or in our scheduled quiet times.

But in your eating and your sleeping and your lying down and your rising up.

In your going out and your coming in.

At the kitchen sink and in the carpool pick up.

Through a hectic workday and while you're changing diapers.

Immanuel is reaching in to THOSE mundane places, waiting with delight for you to glance His way. And every time you do, He explodes with joy!

"THEY LOOKED AT ME!
DID YOU SEE THAT?!
THEY WANT TO LOVE ME!
THEY LOVE ME!!!!"

This book is a clustered compiling of mundane moments where God can be FOUND. It is the beginning of a conversation… a connection… so that you, too, can find Him in every season.

So that your eyes would begin to look for Him in the most unsuspecting places.

So that your voice would begin to bless Him in a million familiar moments.

So that your ears would begin to hear His gentle whispers of pleasure and delight over you as you live before His eyes.

What if every moment could be a holy moment? What if the uncreated God is RIGHT HERE? Ready, available, delighted that you would lean into Him as He leans into you?

Will you come on this journey of discovery with me? Join me on this adventure into the secret places of the mundane, this pilgrimage through seasons of the soul until your own eyes become trained to find Him where so many have forgotten to look. Until your own voice erupts from your chest with blessing and adoration over this ever-present God who loves you. Until leaning into Him becomes the natural rhythm of your gait and hearing His whisper becomes your favorite sound.

Come with me…
Let's find Him together…

Love Much,

Nina Landis

A NOTE ON NAVIGATING THIS BOOK:

The rhythm at which this book was written to be consumed is one that matches my personality: spontaneously FREE. There are no rules. There is no order. You can consume as much or as little as you have capacity for in any sliver of any given moment. Maybe ask yourself this question: "What season does my soul seem to be in?" And then turn the pages until you find it; read the titles until your soul responds; wander down the page until you hear the sound of your own heart beating in the stories and words echoing through you. The secret of this book is in the title of this book: SLOW... SACRED... We aren't in a hurry. And neither is The Champion of our souls. May the words on these pages be a map for your wandering heart. May you return to them again and again and remember that He is the available God. He is surely WITH US.

S P R

I N G

SLOW + SACRED

In the face of bleak sky and cold wind, four little snowdrop buds, the first we have ever had here, have sat for the last 2 or 3 days with their chins on the earth – and now today one of them has reared itself up pure and fearless on its little stalk, with all the promise of the Spring."

6th of February 1903

Lilias Trotter

"The season has changed, the bondage of your barren winter has ended, and the season of hiding is over and gone. The rains have soaked the earth and left it bright with blossoming flowers. The season for singing and pruning the vines has arrived. I hear the cooing of doves in our land, filling the air with songs to awaken you and guide you forth. Can you not discern this new day of destiny breaking forth around you? The early signs of my purposes and plans are bursting forth. The budding vines of new life are now blooming everywhere. The fragrance of their flowers whispers, "There is change in the air.""

Song of Solomon 2:11-13 (TPT)

31

SPRING

It's better than a good stretch upon waking.
It's almost as though you can hear it.
One day the earth is covered in slumber, and then
SUDDENLY,
out of a dreary and lingering death,
"POP!"

LIFE!

Life begins to bud and giggle.
Color whispers on to the grayish scene.
Everything that was quiet and hidden now chatters afresh!
Like a celebration of comrades
gathered to feast and fellowship,
after a long and weary journey.

SPRING!

It's as though the word itself instructs our hearts to rise.
To reach.
To Spring forth with hope and vigor, abundance and
delight.
This is the season where all things seem possible.
Where wonder and stamina,
Courage and creativity,
Glittering light and refreshing rain,
All take front and center stage.

Spring...

It's truly the Great Awakening.

THE BEAUTY OF CHAOS...

Every Spring, after the long, cozy winter has melted away and the new bursts of color begin to appear on the scene, I get this wild hair to completely purge and reorganize SOMETHING!! And every year, the circumstances surrounding the situation reveal the same truth:

The path to more order and simplicity is often full of chaos and mess.

We pull out all the bits and bobs, rethink, reevaluate, and then reset. Projects of "fixing up" require tools for doing so, and then those tools need a home in which to wait for the next project. Reorganizing a cabinet or an office space means you must UNDO it before you can redo it.

This spring was like the many before it. Only this time, while I was staring at the overwhelming chaos of undoing all around me, I heard the gentlest whisper inside my soul:

"This is what your heart looks like."

The truth is, if we want growth and healing, if we want to change and

expand... we must first embrace our
mess.
To find roots, we end up getting dirt
everywhere.
To cultivate order requires taking it
all apart, examining every individual
piece that needs a place to rest, and
then creating a system in which to
rest it.

Even though the "unfinished work"
can feel embarrassing, I'm learning
to embrace the mess of my own
heart.
The mess of other human hearts.
A little more, every day, I'm learning
that healing, wholeness, order, and
space to breathe are just on the other
side of this current chaos.

My confidence is growing in a God
who is able to bring beauty from
ashes, life from dust, and order from
chaos.

A God who isn't finished yet.

Holy Contemplation:
Today, as you examine the landscape of this heart you are unpacking, do not
be dismayed. This is not the end of the story... You know the One who orders
your messy soul. He never gets it wrong, and He always finishes what He
starts. Whisper these words to Him with me: "You can have my messy heart
today. I trust your good work in me."

FINDING OUR FUEL...

We recently hiked a rather challenging mountain as a family, a vigorous trek up to the most stunning rush of water pouring out of the rock and plummeting into the raging river below. I needed to get as close to that roaring water as I possibly could. I wanted to feel the spray on my face, the reverberation drowning out all other sound, the tingling in my legs that comes when you've pushed them hard and now you're standing on the edge of something powerful.

As I stood in that vulnerable place, hands stretched up to the sky so my body could soak in the fullness of every drop, I felt that little pull: a whisper in my heart from my oldest and kindest Friend.

I've always been a bit of a wild wanderer, getting antsy after extended times of taking in the same scene. Marriage, motherhood, and pastoring have tamed me in so many significant and valuable ways, but my lens for the world hasn't changed much. I still take it in with fire in my eyes. I still process it out with fire in my mouth. That is just my design.

I've learned to release my fire in containers now, with beautiful boundaries that help it to be held, seen, and known—as opposed to spewing it without restraint. But the fire is still fire, and it must be released. I finally stopped apologizing for it and

36

started learning to wield it many years ago. Yet despite my most intentional efforts, it occasionally gets spewed instead of packaged and delivered.

Passion probably should have been my middle name. There is simply always scenery to drink in, rivers that resonate, mountains to conquer, hearts to discover, humans to love deeply... these are all fuels to the ever-growing flame inside my soul.

But I have learned they are not the source.

They point me to Him, but they could never replace Him, nor should they ever be confused for Him.

We all require fuel. We must remember to find our fuel. And we'd be wise not to confuse the products of it for the source itself.

I think humans are prone to the frenzy of fuel pursuit.

It's like we wake up some days and realize we're starving or desperately parched: we feel our fire going out. But I don't think it has to be that way. I think we have access to a steady kind of fuel in all the mundane moments of our lives. We don't have to conquer a mountain to find it—although sometimes I am certain the mountain helps.

The source of energy that we pull from that mountain, that relationship, that adventure, that book we're reading while we drink our tea in a cozy corner by the fire... THAT energy has a name! And the source of that energy is ever-present. Always available. Willing to share. And NEVER runs dry.

What if we got our fuel from the source Himself instead of the product of the source? Then all those frenzied moments of feast or famine could turn into a comfortable rhythm of delight. Our NEED could be satisfied, leaving room for our joy to be fulfilled.

There is a Man with eyes like a flame of fire
He holds the source of all our deepest desires
Creation is whispering the sounds of His song
But He is the place we all truly belong

The craving of our soul
The anchor of our hearts
He is where we end
He is where we start

If you're feeling empty, dry, or without grace
Come to the fountain, behold His face
All you have need of His hand will provide
He's always been faithful, the Source of all life

Prayerful Meditation:
Jesus, I acknowledge today that you are the source of fuel for my soul. I
recognize my tendency to feed my heart with inferior pleasure and overlook
you as my daily bread. Today, I'm asking you to become my rhythm. I'm
turning my eyes to your eyes, beholding your face, feasting on your word,
standing in your grace. Lift the light of your countenance upon me... Jesus,
sustainer of all things... sustain me today.

DOLLS + DIVINE LOVE...

For over a year, my firstborn daughter, Aidah, saved every penny she was gifted or earned to buy herself her very own American Girl Doll. We researched the types of dolls, how much each one cost, which one she really wanted, and asked all the experienced American Girl Doll fans to tell us all we needed to know about this very special investment.

Finally, when we were certain she had all she needed, we planned a special trip to the city to make it happen. Before we got on the road, I asked the kids to pray for our trip. Aidah, only seven years old at the time, prayed that everyone in the store would be "really nice" and that "something special" would happen.

While we were in the store, an employee approached us to see if we needed any assistance. Aidah was feeling a little disappointed because she thought she had saved enough money to buy the doll AND take her to the hair

salon (yes, there is a doll hair salon—
who knew?!). But she had just enough
to get the doll and nothing more. She
very sweetly explained this to the
woman, and, honestly, I awkwardly
laughed off her childlike transparency.
I was a little embarrassed that she
didn't have "ENOUGH."

Well, the next thing I knew, this
beautiful woman was blessing Aidah
with a free hairstyle for her new doll!
It included ribbons, a spray bottle
(which she went out to her car to get,
and personally gifted to Aidah), and
a whole lesson on how to care for her
new doll's hair. I watched Aidah's eyes
sparkle with wonder. I saw this sweet
sense of responsibility that comes
when you've worked really hard for
something, and you are holding the
reward of that hard work in your arms.
My eyes welled up with tears as I
realized that "something special" she
had prayed for was happening in that
moment.

After over twenty years of loving Jesus,
I am still overwhelmed sometimes at

how acquainted He is with us. How this creator God can care so deeply for us that these little prayers we pray, which have nothing to do with the world turning but everything to do with our hearts learning the deep wells of His attentive love, become the cares of HIS heart.

I don't understand it, honestly. I can't reconcile an eternal God getting involved with such a temporal request, but the mystery still moves me to tears every time.

He's not distant.
He's not apathetic.
And yet He's the definition of power and creation and life.
He bends down to the dust over and over again to meet our flesh with His divinity.
He whispers into our mundane that He is present and passionately in pursuit of us.

Helping my daughter recognize this unmatched King we serve, well, that was MY "something special."

Holy Contemplation:
What if we look for Him in the temporal moments unfolding around us today?
Do you know that the movement of our hearts toward Him is more precious
to Him than all other things? He is the God who bends down to the dust. He
is the God who desires deep friendship with us! Where is He bending in your
life today? Where is He inviting you into deeper friendship? What if we lean,
with great intention, into His whispers? And then... respond with praise!

WHEN GARDENS SPEAK...

I've spent the good part of this last year tending my little garden, and tonight I feel overwhelmed by its parallels with life. The natural things really do speak of invisible things.

When we showed up to this little home in the hills, we found a half-built fence and rocky ground. I was dreaming of a flourishing garden and determined to find the most economical way to accomplish it.

In many ways, as I labored through this process in the natural, I was wrestling over the condition of my own heart in the invisible places—talking with God through MY process as I cultivated the garden process. What I dreamed it could be and the reality of its current condition were two completely different things.

When I finally sowed the seeds, after SO MUCH preparation and intention, they didn't follow their traditional pattern of germination. I thought, "Man! All this work for nothing! What did I do wrong?" But then, one day, I walked up to those formerly barren boxes, and—all over the garden—fresh life was bursting out of the ground.

You see, unforeseen weather had delayed the germination process. But when the temperature was just right... explosion! I've battled some pests, struggled with water ratios, and had to stay on top of this garden every day to get it to this point... but WOW! If only you could see it now! Brimming with fruitful life, spilling over my raised beds, vining over my arched trellises! "Abundant" is the best word to describe the vision I see.

Tending the garden of our hearts is often the same.
We put in so much work and think, "Man, was all
that for nothing?" But we plant, and we water, and
God gives the increase.

Don't give up on tending that garden of yours. Don't
let unforeseen circumstance convince you to forsake
the process.
Wait on the Lord and HE will renew your strength.
Wait on the Lord, and you will never be put to
shame.
Don't be deceived for one minute that waiting is an
idle work.
No, my friend... You plant, you water, you fight off
the pests, and THEN God gives the increase.

A beautiful friend of mine has sung, so many times,
as a whisper of His heart to mine: "Don't give up,
don't give in, if you don't quit... you win."

Now, I'm singing it to you...
Don't give up.
Don't give in.
If you don't quit... you win.

Prayerful Meditation:
God of the harvest, the garden of my heart is desperate for you. I have tended
to the places that I know need attention; will you show me the places where
work still needs to be done? Reveal the weeds. Catch the foxes that spoil the
vine. Eradicate every pest that tries to devour the good fruit. And water me
well with your Word. Jesus, will you bring increase from this heart of mine?
Come into your garden and make it abundant with life.

NOT THE AUTHOR...

Sometimes, you see your kids, and it feels like you REALLY see them. Like the light shines in a dark room and illuminates every distinct feature for just a minute.

Our children are these little novels being poured onto a crisp, clean page every day. They are this adventure story unfolding right before our eyes. Like an audio book that you just want to keep driving to hear the next part, but at the same time you want to repeat the last chapter because it was that good!

Some parts of the story can be hard to get through. As you read it, you're thinking, "I don't really love this part." But you know if you keep reading, it's going to get better. Just one more page.

I think the wild part is when you realize that you are contributing to the story, but you aren't the author. And parts of the book were written long ago, and they shouldn't be

46

changed at all... just unwrapped a
little more. Like when you read a
good quote and you want to marinate
on it for a while in order to digest all
the richness packed into every word.

I'm being reminded this week
that I'm not the author. I'm not the
finisher. I'm just an editor that really
believes in the story and wants it to
be the BEST story it could possibly
be. And sometimes... being the editor
is hard and tedious. But these stories,
oh man, they're going to be worth the
read!

Every good book needs a good editor,
and the Author knew what He was
doing when He picked you for the
job!

Prayerful Meditation:
Father, as I move through the responsibilities of each role with which you
have entrusted to me today, whether that be my children, my co-workers, my
students, or anyone you have given me influence over, will you gently remind
me that I am not the Author? Will you strengthen my heart and mind to be
a passionate editor who ultimately trusts and surrenders the story and all
its outcomes to you? I yield to the sovereignty of your every word and the
graciousness of your trusting companionship. Amen.

HITTING THE TARGET...

The other day, I was watching my eight-year-old wind up his sling shot, take his aim at a target, and release a rock into flight. His little tongue caught the wind on the right side of his mouth while his furrowed brow did all the heavy lifting. It got me thinking… learning how to hit the target—isn't that the ever-developing journey of our lives?

At first, hitting the target feels awkward, disorienting, like we are barely maintaining our balance. But over time, if we are diligent, intentional, if we keep working at it, we get better. We hone in on our weaknesses. We tweak our instabilities, lay our insecurities aside, and choose to press on. Determine that we will not give up.

Until hitting the target becomes as familiar as breath.
Pull back, release.
Breathe in, breathe out.

I had a long talk with one of my kids recently about determining to do hard things. To not give up just because it doesn't come naturally or because it feels awkward at first. I feel like there is an awakening happening in hearts all around me right now. A recognizing where we have grown weary in pursuit of hitting the target. Where we have laid down our tools, our instruments, our giftedness or anointing… and fallen into a lull. A stupor.

At some point, while we were sitting on that curb or that bench or that back side of a wilderness, we forgot that we were actually designed to hit a target

with our breath of life.
And we convinced ourselves that it was all a
misunderstanding.
The difficulty caused us to determine in our minds
that we must have gotten it all wrong.

But now, suddenly, our fingers are finding the bows
we laid down.
The forgotten sling shots.
Our eyes are clearing from the teary fog, and our
vision is locking on to that target again.
And this little glimmer of a whisper, a hope… it's
rising in our spirit! Just enough for us to make a
choice.

Will we sit on the bench, or will we stand and take
aim?
Will we use the tool or gift we've been given?
Will we face the vulnerability of not being great yet,
for the possibility of hitting the target of our lives?
Will we consider that God can use whatever is in our
hands? Whatever is in our hearts?

It's time for waking up, my friend.
It's time to give it another go.
It's time to load the bow.
It's time…
to hit the target.

Prayerful Meditation:
Holy Spirit, I acknowledge that I got bogged down with disappointment
somewhere along the way. I stopped believing my design, my life, was a
significant part of your story. I stopped asking you, "What's my target?" So,
I'm asking you today... Father, what were you dreaming about for this breath
of life I call my own? What is in my hand? What do you want to use from my
little life to advance your kingdom on earth, as it is in heaven? My Spirit is
willing, you know my flesh is weak. But I will put my trust in YOUR ability to
use whatever is in my hand. Train my hands, God. Train my heart... to hit the
target.

IN PLAIN SIGHT...

We stole away to the mountains
and they sang to us of His majesty

I saw Him in the twinkling eyes of my
children
I heard Him in the laughter of my friends
I beheld Him in the wonder of the sunset
I found Him in the whisper of the wind

He's not so far away, you know?
He's closer than our breath
Longing that we might look for Him
Aching that we lean in

He hides Himself like precious treasure
Kings and queens will search Him out
But this gold is not reserved for the clever
Simple devotion is how it's found

It's hidden in the mundane places
It whispers gently when we draw close
Longing deeply to be discovered

Prayerful Meditation:
Oh humble, available, accessible King, help me recognize you in the in-between. The familiar places where I thought you wouldn't be. From the mundane moments, you are whispering to me. I want to search for you like precious treasure. In my going out and coming in. Help my eyes behold you today. Help my ears to listen.

KAYAKING IN THE RAIN...

Do you ever find your heart fainting a bit on this wild journey called "faith"? To push past what's expected and jump into the unexpected can sometimes feel like the most ridiculous position in which to live.

I've always been a craver of pushing across that line. But I've found, as I get older, and as my family grows, it gets harder and harder to stay in an active place of faith. Of crossing over from comfort to courage.

My incredible husband swept me away on a little 24-hour getaway to a cabin by the lake this week. He knew when we got there that I REALLY wanted to go out in kayaks on the water! But shortly after loading our bags into the cabin, it started to rain. With deep disappointment I looked at him and said, "Well, I guess we can't go now." He looked at me with a little smirk on his face and said, "Why not?"

Friend, something happened in my heart at that moment! I realized I'd been allowing the rain of life to decide for me what I do next. My adventurous heart had gotten so bogged down by what was "expected" that I'd forgotten how to jump off that cliff of faith into the unexpected.

We launched those kayaks into the water.
In the rain.
Mostly all alone because... who does that?
And do you know what?! It was glorious! Better than
I expected.

I'm sure there were moments made more challenging
by the wind and rain, but the exhilaration of the
unexpected and unknown completely eclipsed the
struggle to get there. I was beaming from ear to ear
the whole time.

So, if you were looking for permission to do the
unexpected with God, imagine me smirky-smiling at
you right now when I say, "Why Not?"

Go ahead and hope.
Go ahead and reach for the unseen.
Go ahead and walk by faith... not by sight.

Holy Contemplation:
What are the rains or circumstances that are currently dictating how you
respond to life? Where is one area in your life today that you could take an
intentional step from comfort to courage? From fear or familiar to radical
faith? What if we do it together? Let's step out of the boat and meet Him on
the water today.

FATHERS + SUNSETS...

The tears poured down my cheeks as I stopped to turn my face to the sun one last time before it dipped down beneath the ocean. "Thank you," I whispered into the wind. "Thank you that you are ever present. All around me. In it all. I really do love you. Help me... love you more."

I breathed deeply of the crisp wind as it filled my lungs afresh and, wiping the tears from my chilled face, I ran to catch up to the bubbling chatter of children's voices as they raced after their father.

He was leading the way.
Charting the path.

They trust him the way I want to trust God. Every breath. Every giggle. Every footstep. Every tear. Every instruction can be held confidently in His care.

I think, just maybe, there isn't a soul in the world not craving a father who can be trusted. A good father, whose arm is not too short and who deeply delights in his children. I'm one of the lucky ones—I know a few. But there are still none who can compare to my heavenly Father.

In all the mundane moments of our lives,
He's whispering to us of His nearness. I
just imagine Him, leaning off that throne
of His, peering wide-eyed with a smile
on His face, whispering the simplest
phrase… "Do you see me?"

Are we paying attention? In the sunsets,
in the sunrise, in the meadow, in our
children's eyes… every fleeting thing
testifies of a GOOD Father.

Sometimes He's not in the wind.
Sometimes, He's not in the storm.
Sometimes, He whispers from within and
it's up to us to listen, to adore.
To hang on every word.
To write it on our souls.
To be still… and to know.

Holy Contemplation:
Today, will you listen for Him with me? Will you look for Him in the laundry
room or at the grocery store? Will you watch for His reflection in the water
and breathe deep of His fragrance in the wind?

It's not as mystical as you might think. Start by finding something beautiful
around you. It could be a tree in bloom, your child giggling, or something
else that just makes you smile. Take 30 seconds to truly behold that beautiful
moment. Breathe deeply and slowly. Then… just wait. I promise you He's
speaking… let's give Him some time today and listen.

PESTS + PERSISTENCE...

It's been an interesting year for my garden: lots of pest battles that caused delays and resulted in re-sowing multiple times. After I finally figured out what was destroying my sprouts, eradicated that problem, and celebrated the long-awaited healthy growth, a gopher chewed through the wire base of our beds in three locations and took out four more healthy, fruiting plants!

It's been a battle! But it makes every piece of fruit more precious when you've had to fight for its growth.

It's interesting to me how my garden seems to regularly reflect my personal season. I've been in the fight of my life against a myriad of destructive pests, and every glimmer of healthy growth has been so precious to me.

The garden of our hearts is worth careful stewardship, but a casual approach will leave us devastated and fruitless.
We must be diligent, watchful, intentional, and invite the Lord to instruct us in His strategy.
And THEN, even after all of that, the enemy may still try to sneak in and rob us.

It's at THAT moment that we have a choice.
Will we cling to what is good?
Will we dare to hope again?
Will we savor every victory and continue to do the
work of protecting the healthy growth that remains?
Or will we throw up our hands in defeat, leave the
garden unattended, and let the enemy devastate what
remains?

Now is not the time to neglect our gardens. To throw
up our hands in weary defeat.

Now is the time to steward with even more diligence
the precious growth that remains. To be increasingly
watchful. Increasingly attentive. Increasingly
obedient.

Keep going, friend! Don't give up!
A harvest is coming.
And the fruit is profoundly precious.

"Catch the foxes for us, the little foxes that spoil the
vineyards, for our vineyards are in blossom." Song of
Solomon 2:15 (ESV)

Prayerful Meditation:
Father, you are The Vinedresser. You show us how to care for the places
of our hearts that need nourishment, protection, and growth. Holy Spirit,
will you help us tend the garden of our hearts today? Show us any area of
compromise that we have allowed and protect the fruit of our hearts with
your Word... your truth. Amen.

"IF THOU ABIDE WITH ME"

I've been crying a lot this week—not tears that are filled with ache, but tears that are filled with gratitude. On this journey of love and obedience, the road has NOT been gentle or straight. And yet, when I look back over the steps we've taken, somehow, some way... He always writes the most beautiful story!

This time last year, we were literally homeless and floating from house to house with nearly all our earthly possessions crammed into the back of a pickup truck. My heart was baffled, battered, wrestling to reconcile how saying "yes" to God was costing us SO much! Can I say that out loud?

Sometimes obedience is profoundly costly. It costs your reputation, it costs your pride, it costs your comforts, your tears, and your children's tears. But what I CAN tell you... without a shadow of a doubt and with almost twenty-five years of practice under my belt, are the SAME words that poured out of King David all those years ago...

"I was young and now I am old, yet I have NEVER seen the righteous forsaken or their children begging bread" Psalm 37:25 (NIV, emphasis added).

Today, during our home school lesson, we were reading the words of an old hymn, and I was struck with overwhelm as my tears began to pour again…

"I fear no foe, with Thee at hand to bless
Ills have no weight, and tears no bitterness
Where is death's sting?
Where, grave, thy victory?
I triumph still, if Thou abide with me"

He's what marks the difference between despair and
hope!

He's what bridges the chasm between defeat and
victory!

He's the definitive spark of light in the face of deep
darkness. There is no shadow in Him.

Wonderful counselor,
Prince of Peace…
MIGHTY GOD!

HE. NEVER. FAILS!

Prayerful Meditation:
If thou abide with me… Oh Jesus, teach me to abide. Teach me the power of
this position. Clinging to the rock that is higher. Hoping in the power that is
greater. No matter the circumstance, the mountaintop, or the valley low…
teach me the way of knowing and being known. Steady my heart when the
storm is raging, blow on my heart when the fire is waning. Abide with me. Oh
God, teach me to abide in thee.

A GOOD GIFT....

Many days, at the start of our home school, I ask the kids to invite the Lord to speak directly to their hearts. Something really specific.

And then we wait.

(This is often NOT profound and regularly results in their creative brains changing the characters' names from a movie they saw and then saying that is what God said.)

After quietly reading my Bible for a bit, I began to journal my prayers, as I often do. Do you ever wrestle with wanting your life to actually matter? You know, wanting all the works of your hands to not just be for the sake of existing or surviving but legitimately poured out in a way that's pleasing to God, that changes the planet? Well, that was the nature of my conversation with Him that particular morning. I ended my writing with,

"I just want it to be a good gift to you... my whole life, every detail."

Now here comes the wild part. I then asked the kids what they heard from God. Aidah, only seven years old at the time, turned her journal to a picture that she had drawn and said, *"This is you singing to Jesus, Mama. And God wants you to know that when you do that, it's a GOOD GIFT. And that after you do it, he's going to give you His word."*

I'm sharing this vulnerable story because I want to remind you that God is a God who HEARS. He's acquainted with us in ALL our ways, and He listens to the smallest of ponderings. He leads us so gently through every question and every wrestle. Not because we need to be puffed up or validated in any way, but because He wants to be in it... with us.

In John 17, Jesus prayed this passionate prayer to the Father that we would be WITH HIM where He is. He is not looking for employees to execute His master plan on the earth. He's looking for a counterpart to stand beside Him, to know His heart, to be WITH HIM.

We can't be afraid to be raw with Him. To ask the hard questions and wrestle through the confusing parts of life. He's longing for conversation, and we think we have to polish it up first or make it sound super holy before we start communicating. That's simply not true.

Scripture is clear that when we draw near to Him, He draws near to us. So, whatever your wrestle today, whatever your questions, ask them!
Tell Him!
Because He's the God who hears.
He's the "WITH US" God.

And every detail of our seemingly insignificant lives is ever before His eager and perfectly loving eyes. He's going to respond, friend. Not because we're qualified or have done a single thing to earn it...

but because we're where He wants to be.
We're WHO he wants to be with.

Let's draw near to Him today. Honestly and vulnerably. Watch for Him, as He draws near to us.

Holy Contemplation:
Sometimes I hold His truth and my experience in tension before Him. And in
His kindness, He bends down from celestial thrones and holds them with me.
Because if there's anything I know... it's that He's not the God who leaves us
alone. What if we lift those tensions up to Him today? See if He doesn't bend
down in His holy compassion for our fragile frames and gently help us hold
them. You're not alone, brave heart. We are NEVER alone.

FAITHFULNESS...

So take my yes and break it open
Until it grows into a tree
Of faithfulness
Faithfulness

I don't have to understand
How death leads to life
Just don't let me compromise
Your plan

'Cause faithfulness matters
When the spring rain is delayed
Faithfulness matters
When I'm plowing through my pain
Faithfulness matters
In the prayers of the saints
'Cause FAITHFUL
is your name
FAITHFUL
is your way

EMERALD MEADOWS + GRATITUDE...

When we lived in Northern California, there was this hidden, wondrous gem about forty-five minutes up the mountain from our house. We didn't know what to expect the first time we visited, but all the locals told us we needed to take the trip.

When you first arrive, you pull into a dirt parking lot with cabins all around. No real views—just dirt and cabins. I thought, "What in the world? Why did our friends say this place was so amazing?"

We started up a dirt path that led straight into what felt like a landslide waiting to happen. We were huffing and puffing and thinking, "What's the big deal?" That's when it happened. We rounded the corner of landslide mountain (that's not its real name, but just go with me), and stretched out before us was the most breathtaking scenery we had ever beheld.

Imagine: to the right, a bubbling brook of crystal-clear water and multicolored river rock. Straight in front, a stretched out, billowy blanket of emerald green grasses waving in the breeze. Towering behind, a majestic mountain, kissed on its peaks with little pillows of snow.

It. Was. Stunning.

The moment we came upon this meadow, my daughter Aidah began to giggle. It started like a slow, little bubble, and then, without warning, she started running through the field with squeals of joy. It took me all of about two seconds to shout, "Same, baby girl! SAME!"

I raced into the open space with her, and we laughed our way through a breathtaking blanket of emerald green. Suddenly, pausing with a sigh, I threw my hands in the air and breathlessly declared, "Jesus, you make beautiful things! Oh, how we LOVE you!" My precious seven-year-old, dawned in lace, ruffles, Vans, and a Patagonia cap, responded, "Yeah! You DO make beautiful things!"

As we were walking back, my three-year old's heart overflowed, "Thanks for bwinging us here, mom and dad."

It was a beautiful day I will never forget! My children, again, were teaching me how to hold my heart in a place of wonder and delight.

Did you know that the words "joyful," "joy," or "rejoice" appear a total of 430 times in the English Standard Version of the Bible?

Sometimes... I think we just need to take our cues from the children in our lives and run free with laughter bubbling up from our toes. And then, when we've giggled it all out... say "thank you" to the One who deserves it.

Holy Contemplation:
As you meander through your day today, what if you postured your heart to
look for the beauty, the wonder, the majesty of the moment? What if you let
the giggle arise? What if you allowed yourself to be swept up in the liberty of
delight and then... with great intention... turn your heart to The Creator and
whisper, "Thank you"? Let's try it! Are you with me?

A GREAT TEACHER

Our history lesson today still brings me to tears. It's been many years since I heard the words, "our nation has been attacked." Many years since I watched the screen with thousands of other stunned Americans. I remember the gasping, the tears, the prayers as we helplessly watched the twin towers crumble that tragic day of September 11th, 2001.

I shared a memory with my kids of watching masses running away while a few medics, officers, and firefighters ran toward the disaster. The tears rolled down my face as I talked about the kind of courage—the kind of humanity—that chooses to run toward disaster to save others, instead of away to save themselves. I challenged them to be that kind of human. That kind of brave. And then we gathered around our flag and earnestly prayed for our nation.

There are a world of beautiful and not-so-beautiful differences and opinions about everything from politics to the food we eat. But on that day, we weren't divided. No one was ungrateful for prayer. Everyone was grieving... together.

Today we prayed for unity, for a fear of the Lord to return to the Land, and for wise, brave, noble, God-fearing leaders to take their place in our nation.

I prayed for those four little hearts around my table. That they would become those kinds of leaders. That they wouldn't just complain about everything they disagree with from behind their electronic devices, but instead, they would have courage and run in the direction that saves people! That they would love their neighbors as themselves. That they would truly be the fragrance of Christ on the earth.

Jesus showed us first.

In the face of defiance and depravity, wickedness and rage, He ran in the direction that saves people. He got down in the dirt with us. He bore our grief, and He carried our sorrows. He showed us what laying down your life for your brother looks like. Then, He invited us to take up our cross and follow Him.

I want to be like Jesus.
I want my children to follow His lead.
In a world full of selfish ambition, may we learn from the Greatest Teacher of all…
to wash feet, to bend down to the dirt, and to lay our lives down for each other.
Love looks like something.
I've seen it.

Prayerful Meditation:
Jesus, your ways are not our ways. Teach us your ways.
Jesus, your thoughts are not our thoughts. Teach us your thoughts.
And when the world around us rages to serve ourselves, store up for ourselves, fight for ourselves, think only of ourselves, show us your narrow way again. The way that leads to life. That holy way of love. We want to be like you, Jesus. Help us!

THE SERIAL LISTER...

I'm an avid lister by nature. But my lists are astronomically long. I'm like a serial lister. And then I label the list something impossible like, "To Do This Week," but it has 180 tasks on it. My husband says my "weekly" lists should become "yearly" lists because that would be more realistic.

The danger of serial listers, like myself, is that it's not just that we're always on to the next thing, but while we're on our way to the next thing, we add five more things to our already impossible list. And then our brains become a perpetual swirl of always being behind and never having enough time! Am I the only person like this?! Tell me I'm not alone.

But lately... in all this uncertain, inconsistent, unpredictable life we're living, I've found myself whisking right past the sweetness because of my impossible to do list. It takes real work for me to be present. To turn off my brain, to open my ears, to look with my eyes, and to quiet my spirit long enough to actually SEE this beautiful, precious, fleeting window I'm living in. I feel like Paul in the book of Romans when he said, "what I hate I do" (Romans 7:15 NIV).

I don't want to miss this! I don't want to waste it! I want to be fully in it, snuggling the sweet little bundle of sweaty toddler on my chest and breathing in her smell of earth and leftover jelly from lunchtime. I haven't just been missing moments with my kids, I've been neglecting moments with my Maker. Can you relate to any of this?

Here's my public plea to myself and any other serial listers out there:
Can we just slow down?
Let's breathe deeper.
Let's move slower.
Let's look longer.
Let's listen more intently.
Let's lay down our impossible lists and embrace the beautiful, adventurous, holy life blooming right in front of us.

Prayerful Meditation:
Oh, present God, you are the master of presence. You said that in your presence there is FULLNESS of joy. Will you teach us the way of presence? Will you steady the frenzy inside our souls to recognize the quiet gift of this moment, this day, this breath of life we're living? Give us this day, our daily bread...

75

PRACTICAL BEAUTY...

Last year the kids convinced me that flowers in the garden were just as practical as fruits and vegetables. They pressed into me with persistence, explaining that they were PRACTICAL because they added beauty to our home, and beauty makes us happy. I tried to resist them, but they would not relent.

Truth be told... they made a very good point. So, I reluctantly agreed to designate ONE whole precious raised garden bed to JUST flowers (this was a big step for my very frugal and intentional personality that works hard to make every space and food stretch to maximum capacity!).

What followed, though, surprised me immensely. I found myself, every few days, moseying up to the garden to trim a fresh bouquet. Every bloom, as it formed and opened, whispered to my heart to remember to open. Every cluster of color adorning my table, reminded me of the Master Artist who fills the world with beauty just for the pleasure of watching us delight in what He's made.

As the children walked by the table and "oo'd" and "ahh'd" at each colorful and fragrant display, I learned that beauty was a very good teacher.

It speaks to us of a beautiful God and what He's like.

It challenges us to observe the fleeting days of life. To savor and to cherish this moment RIGHT NOW.

It tenderly reminds us to open... even if you know that it's the beginning of the end.

Open wide and let the light in.
Drink deep and lift your face straight to the sun.

Straight to the SON.

Well, this year, there are THREE beds designated to
flowers! That's right, I said three.

Practical beauty.

That's what we have decided to call it.

I say it often, but I really mean it. Listen to the
children. Ask them what they think. Why they think
it.

And then learn
how to live
like a child again.

Holy Contemplation:
What might you learn from the flowers? Have you ever considered the
way they lift their faces to the sun? How might you lift your face to the Son
today? Maybe you can ask Him to show you some practical beauty in your
life. Something that whispers of His beauty. Of His rhythm. Of His nature.
Something that reminds you to slow down and behold. To keep reaching and
opening to the Holy light of Love that is found only in Christ. Let's take our
cue from the flowers and open up to let His light in.

"The Lord bless you and keep you; the Lord make his face to shine upon you
and be gracious to you; the Lord lift up his countenance upon you and give
you peace." Numbers 6:24-26 (ESV)

SUM

MER

S L O W + S A C R E D

"To see the Summer Sky
Is Poetry, though never in a Book it lie –
True Poems flee."
Emily Dickinson

"For the sun rises with it's scorching heat and withers the
grass; it's flower falls, and it's beauty perishes"
James 1:11 (ESV)

SUMMER

The scorching sun has reared her head
She has an unquenchable thirst.
All that holds water is under fire,
Desperately seeking refuge from her.

Shade is the friend of all living things.
Rain is the longing of their dreams.
Do not be fooled by her morning glow
By afternoon she unveils a furious show.

The red earth fades to cracks and sand
The fruiting plants blister and make their stand
"Hold on, a bit longer, send roots out wide
If summer lingers too long, there's nowhere to hide"

Thicker skin is our only chance
When the sun sets, that's when wild things dance
The dew of the morning, the reprieve of the night
These are Summer's sweetest delights

Be cautious and slow
Fill your glasses, but know

Summer demands an enduring soul

CONSISTENT WATER...

We harvested our potatoes this week only to discover that two additional towers we had sown grew only half of what we harvested last year. It was so disappointing. The biggest problem? Inconsistent water.

We wrestled with our watering system all summer! The timers kept turning off, the water pressure had issues and wasn't evenly servicing the soil, and there were three different occasions where the water was turned off completely, for days, and we didn't know until after the fact. I remember watching the towers and thinking, "Those aren't flowering the way they should." I knew the lack of blooms meant the potatoes hidden in the ground were not producing the way they did the previous year.

Isn't that just like our hearts? They must be tended regularly. They must be checked on. They need consistent watering and can't be abandoned to familiar routines. There are warning signs along the way that tell us about the condition under the soil. We must pay attention.

I think, sometimes, we abandon our hearts to routine only to discover too late that the routine failed us, just like it failed the Pharisees.
Then the damage becomes difficult—if not impossible—to reverse.

But the difference between our hearts and potatoes (there are many, but just go with me for a minute) is that because of JESUS, Man of Mercy, God of Grace, we can change the watering system at any point and heal the fruit that's hidden in the depths.

We can repent, choose to be diligent instead of relying on the routine or the system, ask for His grace to come and cover our negligence, and, in time, what was lost can be found again. What was damaged can be repaired. What was ruined can be redeemed. And our harvest, the fruit of our hearts, can be bountiful instead of bleak.

But not without intention. Not without recognizing neglect or failed systems and making the changes required by pulling on His love that covers a multitude of things.

My heart needs consistent water.
Your heart needs consistent water.
And what is the water of our hearts, friend?
It's Ephesians 5:26: "…having cleansed her by the washing of water with the word" (ESV).
Let's keep our hearts with all diligence! For out of them flow the wellsprings of life.

Holy Contemplation:

What areas in your life, in your heart, have you given over to familiar routines? Like setting the water system and forgetting to check that it's still working. Consistent water isn't about the routine of something, or the simple discipline, it's about the relationship of checking on the condition of our hearts. Is the system or routine properly servicing the growth of your heart? Or did the water system stop working a long time ago, and you forgot to check it?

What if today, instead of reaching for the television or the internet, the news or social media, we reached for the Word? What if we allowed the Word to start a conversation with the living God? What if we gave that parched heart of ours a big drink of fresh water?

YOU CAN'T FALL IN LOVE...

There are intentional moments of love all around us, but the key is staying attentive to the opportunity and then taking it one step further towards action. A friend of mine wrote a song once, and the lyrics are still ringing in my ears:

"You can't fall in love, you have to build it up, brick by brick..."

In a culture celebrating somewhat impulsive, self-serving love, I think those lyrics need to ring out louder and louder in our hearts. I think a generation needs to know that love costs you something.
That you must fight for it.
Make room for it.
Spend time on it.

Real love has substance. It's built, over time, with a thousand "I'm sorry's" and a thousand more "what do you need's." We must look past the end of our own noses and look long into the needs and desires of those around us.
You can't just fall... you must determine, day in and day out, to build.

I'm sitting here today, admiring the radiant beauty of my favorite flowers, that came as a "just because" but are fragrant with intentional love. I'm certain that we have either dumbed it down or overcomplicated it. We either think love just happens to us, or we think love must be flash points of profound feeling.

Love is built with small, steady, humble, and
intentional acts that communicate effort, awareness,
and a willingness to prefer another over ourselves.

Jesus is the King of this kind of steady love.
We see it in His regular reference to His relationship
with the Father.
We see it in the 33 years of walking as a man into the
crescendo of love's divine moment.

What Christ displayed on the cross was not a flash-
in-the-pan display of love. It was a sacred cathedral
of love that had been built outside the bounds of
time. Just like a wedding is a culminating display
of love, the act of the ceremony does not define its
substance. But the journey that led you to the altar,
and the vows with which you build an altar together
after, are those in-between moments where real love
is BUILT.

Holy Contemplation:
Friend, how will you build love today? What is the brick in your hand?
Where is the cathedral you're constructing? Who is the one you will prefer?
What if we determine to make love seen today? Let's add a brick to the
masterful construction of this eternal and glorious cathedral called Love.

WHEN RIVER ROCKS SPEAK...

There's a little escape, up in the California foothills where we used to live. Nestled up against the emigrant wilderness is this beautiful, quiet place where the river runs gently, the snowcapped mountains peer down at us from their lofty heights, and the meadows of waving green grass lull our breath to the quiet rhythm of wind through their blades.

It's interesting to me: I had been to this exact spot maybe fifteen times, and I had never paused long enough to see the masterpiece of color in the river rocks. One summer visit, I spent close to an hour with my kids and our beautiful friend Amanda, treasure hunting the river rocks for the most unique and exquisite ones we could find. My favorite part was how excited everyone was, even my little one-year-old beauty, every time we found one rock that was just a little bit different than the others.

Isn't it a curious thing how we can look at the same object, maybe even the same person, a thousand times and completely miss the beauty right in front of our faces?! What spoke to me most that day was this: if you held each rock alone in the palm of your hand, it didn't seem so remarkable. But when you arranged them with contrasting colors and diversity? Oh, my goodness! The beauty burst forth like the most elaborate work of art!

Isn't that true about all of humanity? These masterpieces of goodness that we call the human race? The beauty in one another shines even brighter when we stand together. Side by side. Nestled in close without forcing our way to the front or the top.

I was so moved on the riverbank that day. I was fascinated by those river rocks that, at first glance, looked dull and gray, but if you washed them off and clustered them with contrast, their beauty exploded!

We weren't meant to stand alone, friend. We weren't designed to be uniform. We have been fashioned with distinction that becomes remarkably more beautiful when it stands clustered together in holy contrast.

We could look at the landscape of each wonderful human around us and see a vast display of gray, OR we could wash ourselves off in the river of His love, gather in unity, and let beauty—the beauty that can only truly be seen gather together—shine.

We need each other in this little breath of life we're living. That person to our left and the other to our right—their unique designs call out to our unique design. And right there in that place of difference... beauty is born.

That sacred space of cleaning our own hearts before God, being exactly who we were fashioned to be, and then standing confidently together—that is what the kingdom of God looks like. And oh, how stunning it is!

Holy Contemplation:
Today, as we venture out to rub our shoulders with the breathtaking diversity
around us, what if we looked for the beauty in it? What if instead of settling
for the dusty, gray film on the surface, we washed ourselves off in the river of
His love, nestled in tightly with the many contrasting colors around us, and
allowed that master artist to reveal His masterpiece?

THE SELF TRAP...

Created vs. Creator
What gathers up our energy

Do we wonder at the Maker
or pursue our own humanity

Are we chasing down the answers
In the fleetingness of flesh

Are we grasping at the fading
Like liquid truth through mesh

When did the hands that fashioned us
Become our afterthought

And the vessels meant to voyage deep
Settle for anchor at the dock

His heart was always the destination
His wonder, His beauty, His love

And we've made ourselves the fascination

Forgetting that He is more than enough

That all our questions and all our answers
Cannot be found within ourselves

That the glorious wonder of knowing Him
Was always the source of humanity's wealth

The most profound
The most exquisite
The most satisfying destination for us to
visit

Was and is and is to come
Our beautiful Jesus
The magnificent One

Look up, beloved
Your answers are not within

Look up, beloved
Your answers reside IN HIM

STAYING STEADY…

When I was a teenager, I asked a mama I deeply respected, "What is one of your most important parenting tips?" I still remember the strength and struggle in her expression when she replied, "Be consistent." I had NO idea then what a powerful and challenging word of wisdom that was.

In this season of my life, I'm doing my best to savor all the "consistent" parenting required of me, but I often find myself pining after the years that won't feel so constant and demanding.

Are those years even real?

This parenting thing is bigger, more beautiful, more painful, and more glorious than I ever imagined. I live in the tension of being thankfully present, while looking forward with hope to a day filled with more conversations and less rebukes, more celebration of victory and less wrestling of the will. I know I'm going to blink, and these years will feel like a sweet and distant memory. Yet, when you're in the thick of it, sometimes it feels like you're just trying to power through to the next season. Have you ever felt like that?

My mom job was hard work this week. And the week is not even over. But I'm willing to live in the tension of working it out.
Steadiness…
It might be one of the most underrated character qualities of our day.
But if Jesus is a ROCK—a rock that keeps us steady—then surely there is hope that we might learn His way.
That we might become more like Him every day.
If we just stay… consistent.

Prayerful Meditation:
Oh perfect Father, will you give me the grace I need to be consistent today?
To love selflessly. Help me lead humbly, with wisdom, and keep me present to
the joy that comes from being in your presence. Oh, that I would stay devoted
to your presence and that my heart would be sustained in that holy place.

ROAD TRIPS + LOVE LESSONS...

One Summer, our family of six set out on an eighteen-hour road trip across the country: California to Colorado, with glorious national parks in between. I had all the sparkly-eyed ideas of how it would go. This GRAND adventure was going to be the most epic core memory of my children's lives. I got to work, prepping snacks, games, art, toys, songs, audio books. I spent HOURS making sure every minute in that car would be enjoyable.

It mostly went as expected. I found myself delighting over the gasps coming from the back seat with every beautiful rock formation and snowcapped mountain range. We had a running tally of wildlife sightings, and we were all anxious to see whether it would be the bison or the antelope that won. There were very few bickering episodes, quite a few sweet and quiet moments, and lots of learning opportunities.

What I did NOT anticipate, however, was the abundance of blood curdling, sweat inducing, ear piercing baby screams coming from the back seat! Despite all my best efforts, it turned out, six-month-old babies do NOT want to be strapped down to a chair for eighteen hours!

Our best efforts don't always produce the outcome we were expecting, do they? But here is the thing: if I had it to do over, I would still take all that time preparing a way for her, even if she didn't get it. Because even though it cost me, she is absolutely worth that cost. Not because she earned it, but because she is loved. And sometimes, I'm learning, love can be unseen or unrecognized or very underappreciated, but that doesn't negate it as love. It just stretches the human heart all the more to practice giving love away without any strings attached.

Being a parent is this magnifying glass on the condition of our love tank. And we can't possibly love our kids selflessly if we don't remember the Selfless Lover, Jesus.
Talk about being taken for granted!
Talk about a holy work that was completely misunderstood and unappreciated.

But He did it! Not because we earned it, not because we deserve it, but because we are loved.
We are His.
He did it for love.

I've been in a season of surrender, unlike any other I've ever known. And the more I yield to the flame, the more dross rises to the surface of my heart. But it's SO BEAUTIFUL! Because when it rises, it can be removed!

At the end of the day, I want my heart to be like His. I want my love tank to look like His. So, He's welcome to use whatever fire He wants to get it there. That trip, he used a screaming baby who couldn't appreciate the work I put in for her. I wonder what He would like to use today?

Prayerful Meditation:
Holy Spirit, you are the best refiner. Your flame is good even when it hurts. Will you give me the grace today to embrace the flame? Help me welcome the fire that purifies this heart of mine, not resisting the invitation to turn the heat up and let the dross rise to the surface. I'm not afraid of your exposing flame because I am confident that you are for me and not against me. Take this heart and make it gold. PURE. GOLD.

97

A HOLY WRESTLE...

Titus came crashing into our lives as our first rainbow baby, right on the heels of two consecutive, agonizing miscarriages that followed the sudden and tragic death of our three-year-old goddaughter. In the middle of my pregnancy, we were let go from our seven-year pastorate due to a sudden financial crisis.

We had little to no consistent income, two babies in heaven whom I was still grieving, and suddenly had to uproot our lives out of the Bay Area and into the mountains. I was exhausted, confused, disappointed, lonely, and in a state of very real grief.

Follow that with a series of ministry blows over the next several years, mounting debt, and door after door slammed in our faces. Our experience was telling us that God was not for us, that God was NOT good.

The goodness of God.

It's a phrase that, culturally, has become almost flippant, but it is spiritually critical to our human existence. And to be honest,

I feel like I've been in the fight of my
life over it! My son's entire life I've been
wrestling with God over this truth about His
goodness.

I say "truth" confidently because wrestling
over something doesn't negate its validity.
But it does confirm the need for it to be
MY OWN. Not something I read in a book
somewhere, not someone else's regurgitated
words, and not because of someone else's
encounter.

We all have things we believe to be true and
things we believe to be false.
Often times, our circumstances can dictate
our position.
But when it comes to God, and this
particular truth, I have this deep knowing
that my circumstances don't get to dictate
His definition.
And therein lies the wrestle for me.
Because our circumstances, our journeys,
our experiences are REAL.
AND... His goodness is REAL.
Sometimes I can't reconcile both.
And that is just the honest truth of it.

But on this grueling, sometimes exasperating journey, this is the one thing I've become certain of:

God... the Good One... He's not intimidated by our wrestle!
He doesn't scoff at our "working it out."
He doesn't belittle us in the process of discovering and believing the truth.
And our wrestle doesn't make Him insecure!

I would never consciously belittle or reject my five-year-old for trying to wrap her mind and her heart around a profound concept, and, in the same way, God will surely not do that to us.

Jacob wrestled God, and it marked his life in a profound way (Genesis 32).
It got him a new name, a new definition!

So don't let the world tell you to be ashamed of your wrestle.
Because the truth is we are all in the fight of our lives.
The key is not to let go, friends.

Just don't. Let. Go.

Prayerful Meditation:
Oh Jesus, your word tells me that you are GOOD. I believe your word. My
circumstances are trying to tell me a different story, and I can't seem to
reconcile the two. Will you meet me here, God? Will you hold on to me as I
hold on to you today? Don't let me go! I won't let you go.

LABOR OF OUR SOULS...

When we moved to a three-acre stretch of land in Northern California in 2015, we had broken hearts and absolutely no extra money. I remember asking my husband, Ryan, with tears pouring down my face, if there were any way we could make a garden with what we jokingly called "imaginary money." Of course, he twisted himself in pretzels to make it happen because that's how he loves.

"No money" equals "do it yourself with whatever scrap you can find, and make it work." But it was important to me because gardens help me heal.

Something about sowing + reaping. Something about tending + trusting. Something about working diligently with our hands + actually being able to hold the fruit of our labor.

In the ministry world (our primary occupation for the past twenty-plus years), it is often difficult to physically see the fruit of your labor. Yet you LABOR in such a profound way.
I've noticed that many people do not have an accurate concept of just how strenuous, demanding, and costly a primary occupation of ministry actually is.

It is not for the faint of heart.
It is definitely not for the faint of faith.

But gardens? Gardens are simple.

You prepare soil, you plant seeds, you water,
you pull weeds, you watch for pests, and
you respond accordingly. And then... you
wait. And sure enough, even as the sun rises
and sets, fruit forms. Tangible fruit you can
hold and feast on. The fruit of your labor.

Jesus, over and over in scripture, uses the
allegory of gardens to teach us about His
kingdom. About our fragile human hearts.
Our hearts are these gardens.

The soil needs to be cultivated, broken
up, and softened. The seeds need to
be intentionally sown and watered
CONSISTENTLY. The little sprouts must
be guarded. Protected. And they desperately
need the Sun.

We desperately need the Son.

Holy Contemplation:
What if we really made our hearts a garden enclosed? A place for Him alone
to dwell? Our hearts must be kept with all diligence, because from them flow
the well-springs of LIFE. Today, friend, will you wait for the Lord with me?
Will you be strong as you assess the needs of your garden? Will you take
courage as you do the work required for fruitfulness? I am confident, if we
faint not, we will surely share the feast of the labor of our souls.

WHISPERS OF GOD...

Watching my firstborn son as he grows has been one of the most refining and sanctifying journeys of my life. I often find myself praying, reaching with hope, that if somehow I can manage to lead him to those moments where God's whispers seem to break through the noise of our lives, then he'll know the truth.

Moments like the sunrise over the water that's wrapped in the most serene silence and stillness—you're almost unable to speak, but you're filled with anticipation of what's coming.

Or the vigorous climb to the top of a mountain where the air gets crisp, bold, and thin, and the wind strikes against your face like it's waking you up from a deep sleep.

The trickling sounds a creek makes in the middle of a wood when there's no one around but the bees buzzing in the distance, and you can feel your own heartbeat match the rhythm of the bubbling brook.

Those whisper moments where you can't escape from the truth that there's someone so much bigger than you.
Where it's all you can do to just ask the question, "Are you there? Do you know me? What are you like?"
Those windows of the soul, where somehow you just know that you're known.
Where His holy whisper begins to reverberate inside your soul.

I know if I can just lead my son to those sacred
spaces, somehow, that's where he'll grow.
Where the boys turn into men.
Where the busy learn to listen.
Where the weak push through to strength.
Where you meet Him face to face.

Because creation testifies. It tells us a story. It invites
us into HIS story.

The same way Jesus was always stealing away from
the crowds just to be with His Father.
If somehow I can just pass on this custom until he,
too, is known for this custom...

A heart that is reaching and leaning and listening,
always just longing to be with his Father.

That's what I'm dreaming about today.

Holy Contemplation:
Go ahead and quiet your soul now. Breathe in a good, long breath, and let it
all the way out. Close your eyes, and ponder a time when you KNEW there
was someone bigger than you. Can you remember it? Can you feel your heart
beating with anticipation of that exhilarating thought? The thought that you
aren't alone. The thought that you are fully known and fully loved, and it's
the kind of love that you can't and never want to escape from. Let's take time
to remember Him like that today. His love. His availability. His beauty. His
grace. His overwhelming delight in and acquaintance with your frame.

THE FAITHFUL...

I'm looking for the voice of Truth that echoes through His body.

I'm looking for a bowing low in speech, in heart and deed.

I'm looking for the tremble that's found when we've been with Him.

I'm looking for the tears that pour from eyes once dead, now clean.

I'm looking for the evidence that His blood has truly bought us.

I'm looking for His fragrance.

I'm looking for His friends.

I'm looking for the lovesick hearts that ache for His appearing.

I'm looking for the free ones, without fear of man.

I'm looking for the faithful...

Having done all...

STAND.

106

THE GREAT GAP FILLER...

My kiddos are growing faster than I ever imagined possible. Bobbling through this wild life, looking for their place in the intricate puzzle of it all. They discover so much every day that it reminds me to keep up!

Keep exploring,
keep discovering,
deliberately uncovering the beauty and wonder of every single moment.
Push through fear and uncertainty,
laugh often,
and don't be too serious when you make mistakes.

I heard a statistic the other day—how accurate it was, I do not know—comparing how often a child laughs in the course of a day and how often an adult laughs in the course of a day. The difference was substantial enough to take my breath away.

Teaching my children is one of the hardest jobs of my life, and I'm in the constant battleground of, "I'm not qualified, I don't have what it takes, and I'm totally going to mess them up."
BUT, I keep telling them,

"Do your very best, with all your heart, then give it all to Jesus. He'll fill in your gaps and make you great!"

Then, I take a deep breath, and I whisper those same words in the form of a prayer:

"Jesus... come and fill in all my gaps. Help me teach these babes with all my heart. Help me lead them into something great."

Then the tears pour down my face because life is FILLED with these kinds of prayers, and I know I'm speaking to a God who hears.

Oh, how we need Him to fill in all our gaps.

Oh, how we need His gentleness to make us great (Psalm 18:35 ESV).

Holy Contemplation:
Can we trust the Author and the Finisher to write the most beautiful story with our fleeting little lives? Can we give Him our absolute BEST and know that He is the great gap filler? What areas in your life are you trying to hold together all on your own? Stretching our arms to max capacity, knowing you aren't enough to bridge that gap. Invite Him, right now, to that space. I promise you; His arm is not too short.

HOPE THAT IS SEEN

Yesterday, I read a parable from nature about
faith with my children. We talked about how,
"Faith is the substance of things hoped for,
the evidence of things unseen" (Hebrews 11:1
KJV). I asked my kiddos to think of a time that
required faith. Aidah chimed in, "The time
Malachai prayed for someone's deaf ear, and
it opened!" We were immediately thrust into a
tangible example that awakened all our hearts to
a deeper understanding.

"Yes!" I said, "It took HOPE for a God who
heals, for Malachai even to ask in prayer for that
person's healing! And THEN... the evidence
of an unseen God was made manifest in their
healing! In that answered prayer." I watched all
their faces fill with wonder at the connection.
The Word of God, suddenly applicable to their
experience.

Faith is not without substance, friend. Faith is
not without evidence. But we cannot put the cart
before the horse, can we?

First comes the exercise of hope,
then comes the evidence of the unseen.
The cliff jump for the human heart is always in
the hoping.

Hope requires courage. It can look foolish and
without merit.

But hope, friend, if we dare to jump, is met
with the surest evidence of an unseen God who
whispers through the windows of our souls.

He whispers of a whole world that's bigger than
our fear.
A kind kingdom that is more powerful than our
frailty.
A government that rules in love and light.
A Father with open arms and an open heart.
A Son who lays His body down as a bridge to
connect us to His Father and sends His Spirit to
help connect us to His inheritance. So we can be
WITH HIM... where He is.

Some may call it foolishness.
The scripture calls it faith.
But one thing is certain: the first step is in the
hoping.

Prayerful Meditation:
God of all hope, will you renew our sense of hope today? Will you gather
together all the hope deferred and wash it away, replenishing our souls with
fresh courage through the free gift of faith? Will you cause our hearts to hear
the knock, and with courage would we open wide the door to hope... to faith...
to the quickly-approaching EVIDENCE of unseen things? We confess today,
that just because we cannot see them, doesn't mean they are not there. We
trust you to bring evidence to the unseen treasures of our souls. Amen.

111

GOD OF ZION...

I'd been dreaming, for a long time, about hiking through The Narrows, in Zion National Park. You know how you can hear about something, and then everything in you begins to resonate with a longing to move from hearing to experiencing?

I've never really been great at settling for the hearing alone.
Let me touch, smell, behold—
let me experience!

From jumping out of an airplane at 21, to swimming with black tip reef sharks and sting rays in open water, I know that adventure and experience make my heart feel connected to the Creator of it all.
I usually cry.
I always worship.
It's a natural response for me.

So, when the day came to EXPERIENCE The Narrows with my sweet family, my heart was filled to bursting and my eyes twinkled with delight. I'm pretty sure I looked like a little kid at Christmas as we trekked through the frigid water with the rock walls towering high on either side of us.

My baby, Fyn, strapped to my back, my
husband, Ryan, holding tight to the hands of
our two middle kids, occasionally scooping up
the younger of the two when the water got too
deep, and our oldest, Malachai, always charging
ahead. The smile was smeared wildly across my
face, and all our eyes twinkled with wonder.

WHAT.
A.
RUSH!

The contrast, though, was that the season in
which the dream came true was also a season of
deep grief and sorrow.
Loss after loss, betrayal after betrayal.
And right in the middle of all my ache and
disappointment, we stole away on an adventure
for the soul and met with the Grand Creator in
the middle of Zion.

Isn't that just like God?

All my life, I've seen the Lord make a way for
seemingly impossible things.
All my life He's taken the most difficult of
seasons and reached down right in the middle of
it all and kissed my head with His goodness, His

nearness.

I haven't always recognized it, but He's always done it.

God is very comfortable with the dichotomies of life. I think it has something to do with getting our whole hearts? Somehow, living in those tensions draws us into the depths of love, mercy, grace, and truth.

We are not alone in our aches or wrestles, friend. His arm is not too short to rescue us from drowning.

We are seen.

We are known.

We are deeply loved and held and cherished. And we WILL find what we're looking for.

Turns out, I'm on a voracious hunt for the goodness of God.

May we all become voyagers on THAT expedition.

And oh, beloved, may we find what we're looking for.

Holy Contemplation:
Can you think of moments in your life right now, in which the goodness of
God bent down to kiss your head in the middle of your ache or wrestle?
Where can you find evidence that a good God has been near to your heart
this year? Today, as you wash dishes or drive through the carpool line, take
time to remember. Take time to magnify the Grand Creator of Zion. Delight
in Him, right in the middle of your ache.

THREAD BARE...

My youngest was wearing a dress today that belonged to my mama, then my older sister, then me. Somehow, my mama salvaged that dress and gave it to me in a bag of vintage clothes when my first daughter was born. She wore it proudly, and now, after all these laughs and tears, births and deaths, victories and defeats, through many states and cities across the country and finally to this present moment, that dress makes its appearance on the youngest of our family line.

If that dress could speak, what stories would it tell?

Generations... we pass so many things down through the generations. Some things we know about, but some things get woven into our fabric without us even noticing the thread. But after many years, when those garments become threadbare and each string begins to take on a certain distinction, we start to see what the garment is really made of.

I think, maybe, that's when it's time for two things:

A thread examination.
To examine our garments, so to speak. What we put on or carry with us every day without even realizing what it's made of.
If there were toxic threads in your garment, would you want to know before you passed it on to your own children to wear?

A sobering and intentional awareness that we are not only living unto ourselves and this present age.
We are passing something to our children's children.
Every choice we make is a thread in a garment THEY will one day wear.

Let's fashion it with care. With the purest of thread.
With the most intentional stitching.
Let's fashion it to last and remove every toxic thread
that could seep into their skin over time.

We can't ignore the threads anymore.
We can't brush the few flawed strands away and hope
that if we just stitch over it, it won't really impact
anything... or anyone.

Every lasting change starts with a humble but
courageous heart.
Absolutely NOTHING can be lost through thread
examination.
But SO MUCH can be gained.

Over time, if we're willing to do the work with God
and remake any worn-out garment, we'll be able to
fashion it with enduring intention.
Then, with all confidence, we can pass that beautiful
garment from one generation to the next.

Knowing WE did the work so THEY could wear the
peace.

Prayerful Meditation:
Father, I know there are ideas, patterns, or strongholds in my heart and mind
that have been passed down to me through the generations. I don't want to
pass a single thing that is not from you, on to the next generation. I'm asking
you today, like King David, to search me and know me (Psalm 139). To see if
there is any wicked way in me. Then, will you lead me? Oh, Good Shepherd,
will you lead me in that everlasting way? Amen.

WONDERFULLY MADE...

You know what's crazy? After almost thirty years of knowing and loving Jesus, I'm still learning how to abide in His relentless delight.
Freely.
Completely.
His delight IN ME.

Did you know that the Creator of the heavens and the earth, the One who knit you together in your mother's womb and holds the stars in His hands, the One who gave the seas their boundary and commands the morning...
THAT glorious, passionate, fascinating King looks at YOU,
looks at ME,
and His heart is GLAD?!

He drinks in the complexities and creative genius of our frame and boldly declares, "This is VERY good!"

That phrase—"Fearfully and wonderfully made"—rings out over and over in my heart and mind. Reverberating off the fragile insecurities dancing around in my subconscious and becoming the very fabric that is holding my soul together.

Fearfully... meaning: mysteriously complex.

Wonderfully... meaning: exactly that, FULL of WONDER!

Not one human frame is exempt from this eternal declaration.

Not one can escape this resounding identification that echoes through the corridors of history and lands ever so gently, ever so profoundly, into the depths of our being.

Maybe you needed to hear it again today? The way I need to remember it every day.

When you peer into your reflection, tempted to dissect and deconstruct every detail of the frame staring back at you, may you remember your Creator's declaration over you!
May you whisper His words in echoed meditation until they permeate the depths of your being...

"Fearfully, wonderfully made.
VERY good.
The delight of my Father.
Fashioned in the image of a perfect God.
Full of wonder.
Mysteriously complex.
I am GOOD.
Very. Good."

You are good. Very good.

Prayerful Meditation:

God, I struggle to believe that this temporal tent you fashioned is good. I want to believe it! Will you pierce my heart today with a holy revelation of what you FEEL when you look at me? Will you allow me to experience your emotions and thoughts concerning this frame you've fashioned? Will you expose and break off every agreement I've made with a lesser truth? Every lie I've accepted and held in my body? My very. Good. Body. I give you my tongue—that it may not curse what you've made anymore. And I give you my thoughts—that they may only hold the purest ponderings concerning myself, others, and you. Cause your truth to reverberate inside my soul today... let me hear you say it again: "You are very good!"

SIMPLE DEVOTION...

The days have been filled with labor,

but the reward is abundantly rich.

I rest and it helps me remember

That I've been caught up in his-story,

Simple devotion is where love fleshes out.

There's still more to give,

there's love yet to be lived,

and where treasure is held,

there my heart is.

DON'T GIVE UP...

I could feel hope rising in my chest today as we danced across the breathtaking mountainside of Colorado with some of our best friends.

I could hear it like a whisper: "Don't give up."

An invitation to dream again has slipped under our door.

Isn't it curious how quickly we lose the wind in our sails? How often we yield to obstacles and trials as a cancel stamp upon our hearts?

Today, seasons of wrestle give way to moments of delight.
Heartache and disappointment are overtaken by faithfulness and encouragement, and the whispering flame of hope has begun to flicker in our beating chests again.

So, I am here to remind you that where injustice and disappointment has raged against your spirit and fought to tear it down, a still, small voice... a faithful God is whispering over the noise, "Don't give up."

124

Don't give up your hope...

Don't give up your dream...

Don't give up the passions that cause your heart to sing....

You were knit together with great delight

And the keeper of your heart is willing to fight...

To fight for the goodness He wrote through your soul

To manifest His beauty

To make Himself known

Circumstances are ever changing,

But Jesus is ever true.

Hold fast to Him, beloved.

He's holding fast to you.

A U T

U M N

SLOW + SACRED

"As long as autumn lasts, I shall not have hands, canvas, and colors enough to paint the beautiful things I see."
Vincent Van Gogh

Truly, truly, I say to you, unless a grain of wheat falls into the earth and dies, it remains alone; but if it dies, it bears much fruit.
John 12:24 (ESV)

AUTUMN

It happens rather gently
So as not to awaken fright
A slow moving in from the edges
Like a shadow through fading light

There's beauty to be found in the dying
The in-between space where we live
It doesn't have to be tragic
Just a gentle shift in perspective

Look at the trees and their colors
They tremble and yet yield to the wind
In their shedding seasons of plenty
They share beauty that was hidden within

Completely surrendered
To volunteer
To colorfully give way to the falling tears

Autumn reminds us
To cherish the space
Between fruitful harvests
And bitter days

Autumn, like a wise and intentional Sage
Teaching us humility
To die with grace

Courage, dear heart
Learn well from the trees
Beauty is found in the in-between

OUR TEETHING HEARTS...

When we are in pain, sometimes the only thing to do is lean. With all our discomfort, we press our weak frames, desperately, into our safest place.

One cold, crisp morning, when my beautiful, fragile one-year-old was navigating her pouring nose, cutting teeth, and hacking cough pain, I caught a glimpse of this innate human instinct.

She would locate my whereabouts in the house and, stumbling up with her red-brimmed eyes, sniffly nose, and drooling little mouth, she would lean.

All her body weight into mine.

Then I would say, "What can I do to help you, babe?" I knew she was desperately uncomfortable, and I longed to help ease her pain. Then, with such achy tenderness, she would lift her longing eyes to mine and say, "Up, mama. Up!".

After about the fiftieth time (that is not an exaggeration) of gathering her into my arms, holding her tightly against my chest, scratching her delicate back, wiping her runny little button nose, stopping ALL of life's demands simply to be WITH her in her pain, a revelation lighted on me like a blanket of comfort wrapping my weary soul.

That's what WE get to do!

We get to lean our insecure, uncomfortable, aching, and weary hearts into the steady, consistent, dependable comfort of our good God.

Pleadingly look into His compassionate eyes and bid

Him to gather us UP...
into His perspective. UP...
into His safe embrace. UP...
where pain and ache and disappointment are not
emptied or gone, but they are held.
Shared.
Supported by the safest One we know.

And oh, won't He gather us?

Into those everlasting, never weary, oh-so-patient
arms.
Won't He hold us through the pain?
Through the disappointment?
Through...

He will carry us through.

To the morning where mercy is new, hope is fresh,
and pain subsides a bit.

One lean at a time.

He's just waiting for us to lean.

Holy Contemplation:
Today, as you carry your heart through the rhythms of life, will you practice
with me? This holy leaning. This hoping in the strength and steadiness of HIS
frame. No words required. Just a kind of falling into... I bet you'll find that
He desperately longs to gather you...
UP.

THE GREAT LEADER...

"He leads me beside still waters. He restores my soul" (Psalm 23:2-3 ESV).

Do you ever just ache inside for the quietness that can only come in the restoring of your soul? The whisper of peace that sweeps in when reconciliation has worked its way into the very fabric of your being? The kind of knowing that comes when you can FEEL the most comforting presence in all of the universe, and you don't even have to open your eyes to see Him?

Lately I've felt a craving for that kind of quietness, that kind of restoration. Even though I KNOW what accusation sounds like, and I fight from my bones not to give my ear to those lies, sometimes I still lose sight of that sweet restoration that only comes if I

LET.
HIM.
LEAD.

Truth is, I kind of fail at following. Sometimes I charge ahead. Sometimes I wander so far off that His loving kindness really does have to chase me down.

But He DOES.

In His way.
In His time.
And always in His kindness, He chases
me down until I recognize that my soul is
panting.
I need water.
And I need a leader to get me there.
THE Leader.

Sometimes I tire at my own forgetfulness.
But He never grows tired of me. He NEVER
grows tired of you. He just doesn't grow
tired at all.

So, if by chance you are a little bit like me,
and your wrestle has looked a little like
some of these things I've mentioned, He's
coming for you today, my friend. With
all the mercy and loving kindness that He
carries inside of Himself.

And when He gets there... just speaking
from experience... maybe go ahead and let
Him lead?

Prayerful Meditation:
Good Shepherd, my faithful and perfect leader, I'm tired. I've been running
so hard and wrestling so much, and I need you to save me from myself. I yield
today to your kind and patient leadership. I lean into your voice, and I quiet
my own. I don't have the answers, and I don't know the way, but you do. Lead
me, and I will follow.

WHAT DO POTATOES KNOW?...

The year we harvested our first potato towers, I learned that growing potatoes is fun!

It's interesting because there is a whole world of activity exploding beneath the surface that no one can see! First, the plant sprouts; you watch it flower, but you can't see the "fruit." With potatoes (and many other things in life, I think), the fruit is buried deep in the hidden places of the earth.

And here is the most fascinating and oddly encouraging fact about potatoes… Do you know how to tell when the potato is ready?

Everything on the outside—everything you can see with your eyes—dies.
That's how you know the hard, hidden, intricate, unseen work of fruitful growth is complete.

"Man looks on the outward appearance, but the Lord looks on the heart" (1 Samuel 16:7 ESV).

If you were in my garden on that harvest day, you may have found me weeping over potatoes. So often, we spend ourselves tending to what everyone else can see. But what if we were willing to die to that striving after wind? What would happen if we could die to that man-pleasing roller

coaster ride? Well... that's when the real
work could begin.

The description used in explaining this
potato process states that all the energy that
was being spent on the outward plant, now
focuses inward, so the potato can grow to its
FULL POTENTIAL.

How much energy do we spend on that
outward appearance?
How much time and emotion, thought and
strength?
When, really, if we would just die to it, then
our energy could go inward, to the secret
places that are buried deep inside our souls.
And we could tend to those places.
So that the beautiful, intricately-knit-
together hearts of ours might grow to their
FULL POTENTIAL.

In the ever-increasing clatter of our outward
lives, let's do the inward work, friend.
Let's spend our energy on these hearts of
ours.

Holy Contemplation:
What areas of your "outward appearance" can you willingly begin to die to
today? What deep work in your soul is craving nourishment and attention?
Oh, that the Holy Spirit would cause us to reach our FULL potential. Oh,
that we would do the voluntary work of dying to our flesh so that He can.
"I affirm, by the boasting in you which I have in Christ Jesus our Lord, I die
daily" (1 Corinthians 15:31 NKJV).

BEAUTY IN THE IN-BETWEEN...

Our journey with children has been beautiful and blistering, painful and precious. Seven pregnancies. Three babies in my arms, three babies in the Lord's, and one beautiful little girl in my womb.

We all live in the tension of great loss and great victory in this breath of a vapor we call life. And somehow, the ache teaches us to savor the joy all the more.
One of my favorite songwriters wrote a song called, "The Shadow Proves the Sunshine" (Switchfoot). And that couldn't be truer on this journey with our baby girl.

To say that my heart is swelling with gratitude would be an understatement, and to say that it's free from worry and an occasional holding of my breath would be untrue.

But I don't despise the tension, and I'm learning to find Him in the in-between. It's a wrestle... every day... but having counted the cost and having held the reward, I say yes again today.

We are not those who sorrow without hope. It's both/and.
And the mystery of God in the tension of

those places is a mystery I'm willing to sit
with.
To behold,
to wrestle,
to confront and ultimately,
to pull up a chair.

Unanswered questions don't have to be
unasked.
Death doesn't have to be mostly gruesome.
Picture the trees on a crisp autumn day...
there's beauty to be found in death.

New life doesn't have to eclipse the
preciousness of what was before it. It can
stand alone in its beauty and still be held
with tenderness BECAUSE of a cost that's
been counted.. felt... paid.

Whatever your losses, whatever your
tension, there's beauty in the in-between.
Let's hold space for both today.

Permission to sorrow... with HOPE.

Prayerful Meditation:
Abba, I know my grief is not lost on you. I know you hold compassion for
my ache and simultaneously rejoice in my victory. Will you teach me to hold
them both the way you are able to hold them both? Today, will you help me sit
with grace in the tension of the two and find you? Amen.

WHEN DEEP IS CALLING...

I was talking with a friend recently about my tendency to go deep right out of the gate. How I skip surface chatting and dive into the depths of the heart. I have an ongoing joke with friends about how I become the "Debbie downer" of all social gatherings because I end up crying or making someone else cry as I unearth what's REALLY going on in there.

But here's the thing: when I look out at this great big world around me, what I see are little treasure chests of human hearts everywhere. Full of the richest gold and gems and stories, just waiting to be seen, heard, valued, and cherished. I'm always apologizing for my intensity, but I can't seem to turn it down.

As I watched my family dance with the ocean yesterday, I felt all the deep things. Breathed all the deep breaths. And thought to myself,

"Why do we (human beings) hide from the depths?
Why do we tuck it away?
If we were made in the image of a deep, feeling God...

140

we don't have to be afraid of really looking
at those places.
In ourselves AND in each other."

I backed away from a deep conversation
recently and spent the rest of the night
thinking,
"I shouldn't have backed away.
I should have shown her that she was worth
the discomfort of that conversation.
That it was ok to cry.
That it was ok to be vulnerable right there
in that socially incorrect location."

I don't always get it right, this treasure-
hunting-in-human-hearts thing. But the
older I get, the more I'm convinced that
deep is the more natural choice.

We've trained the depths out of our culture.

I think I'll fight to bring it back.

Are you with me?

Prayerful Meditation:
Holy Spirit, you are the one who searches the deep things of God and reveals
them to us. You are the gift that knits us together with the Godhead. You
are alive in me. Will you help me search the deep things of God and men?
Will you save me from being lulled to sleep by the surface culture that I am
currently living in? Show me your way. The way of the deep. Amen.

STACKED...

My Bible

Stacked on his

He's first to rise

And first to dive

Dive into the depths of knowing

Breathing

Holding life

Steady

Inside our souls

Leading through a bending low

In quietness

And rest

We will build our home

When nothing makes sense

When breathing is hard

We stack our Bibles

And we start...

Again

THE LITMUS TEST...

I've been thinking about being right...

You know? That thing that everyone strives after, like all of the time, in every area of life? Mostly because I'm raising four beautiful little hearts, and our regular battle around here is that dispute over who is "RIGHT."

Can you relate? My kids bicker more over this topic than maybe any other topic. But they aren't alone.

The majority of my social media feed these days, the stories I read on the news, the conversations around tables and at parties—it all really boils down to everyone trying to be "right."

"Every way of a man is right in his own eyes, but the Lord weighs the heart" (Proverbs 21:2 ESV).

The thing is... it was never about being right. It will never be about being right. You know what is really being weighed? You know what carries the most clout at the end of EVERY story? You know when our energy and research and disciplines and conversations really start to matter? When we are diving into the business of the HEART.

The battle over our hearts is at an all-time high because, "out of the abundance of the HEART the mouth speaks" (Matthew 12:34 ESV, emphasis added).

So, what's coming out of our mouths most?
It's a litmus test for the condition of our hearts.

What if we worried less about being "right" and
got consumed with being love?
What if we paid closer attention to the weight of
our hearts than the weight of our knowledge?
What if we took the low road of humility and
preferring others, the meek road of mercy and
compassion, instead of shouting and waving our
banners of justification on the mountaintops of
pride?

Pride...

It comes before a fall.

It has ALWAYS been, it will ALWAYS be about
the heart.

So, if our hearts aren't growing in love... then
our "right" will always be "wrong."

I think we've got some work to do.

Prayerful Meditation:
Father, I lay down my fight to be right. I step humbly into the teachable
position of a heart that still has so much room to grow. I'm asking for your
help today. To catch me when I begin to fall into this pattern of PROVING.
Increase my ache to be continually transformed by your great love. Increase
my awareness of my own need for a Savior. Of my own desperate need for
your holy perspective. When everyone was clamoring to be right, you took
off your outer garments and you bent down and washed their feet. Teach me
THAT way. Your way.

145

LOVE IS IN THE DYING...

It had been over three years since we had spent time with my family in Northwest Arkansas. It's crazy how much nephews can grow and grandmas can age in that amount of time. Three years is a long time in childhood and in elderly life.

My beautiful, Sicilian grandmother didn't remember as much as she used to because dementia had been a ruthless thief, but if you asked her to sing a song, tell a story from her childhood, or crack a joke about anything in particular, she was ready and willing to oblige.

Aging is such an interesting thing to watch. It's almost as if we grow from children into grownups and back into children again.

My gorgeous mom had gone from caring for her children, to her grandchildren, to her mother. What a champion of love she is. I was more aware this particular trip than ever of just how costly love is. Watching it sacrifice and pour itself out in a million little ways.

Love is not a flippant thing that sweeps us away or only comes from the overflow of natural response. No, friend... loving the babies, loving the elderly who can act like babies—it looks like it costs you everything! And somehow, in the middle of life, we think love looks like GETTING. Well, I think we might have that wrong.

Love looks like GIVING.

Your time, patience, grace, energy, strength,
hope, courage, forgiveness, humility, surrender,
and repentance.

Real love costs.

It's a cross.

And it's a cross I am willing to bare.

It's a cross I have watched my parents bare.

But we can't bear it on our own, friend. We need
His help to carry it. Real love can only come
from the source of love Himself. We can give it
away only after we have learned to sit with Him
and receive it. We must learn to yield our own
way to His way.

The way of love is the way of the cross.

"Greater love has no one than this, that someone
lay down his life for his friends"
(John 15:13 ESV).

Prayerful Meditation:
*Jesus, you showed us the way of true love. You continue to show it to us over
and over again. Will you bring that holy work to completion in this heart of
mine? Will you give me grace to suffer long, to hope all things, to keep no
record of wrong? Help me love like you love today. Amen.*

147

MARKETPLACE VALUE...

I'm a songwriter, and over the years I've noticed a pattern in the life of many songwriters. They are always in the tension of the song that is written right-the-way through them, and the song that they THINK everyone else wants to hear.

Years ago, I was sitting in a church service on the back row. My heart was deflated and broken because we had just spent our life savings (plus some) to record an album of songs that held my most vulnerable and honest heart cries within their melodies.

We were certain that this creation would be seen and heard, and others would recognize the groan, ache, labor, delight, and creative culmination that we had so diligently poured our ever-loving-guts into. But, as stories of expectations often go, it was received fairly well, but we weren't selling nearly as many as we had hoped.

I was feeling like I missed it.

I failed.

I was wrong.

In that church service, in the middle of his
sermon, the speaker walked straight down the
aisle to that back row where I was sitting. He
pointed his finger at me and locked in with my
eyes and said,

"DO NOT let the marketplace determine the
value of what was formed in the secret place."

I remember those words; they struck like
an arrow to my heart. I began to weep as
I recognized this weight that had so easily
entangled me. This man, he didn't know me. He
didn't know my story. But the Spirit of God in
him knew it. And He met me and marked me on
that back row.

The value of our song (or our art, our work, our
words… whatever your design and expression of
that design), is not and never will be determined
by what a world full of fickle hearts have to say.

Our song—the value of our song—comes not
from what it is, but WHO it's for!

Don't forget who's listening.

Don't forget who you were fashioned for.

Don't forget that what you do in secret, the Lord will reward openly.

When you pray, when you sing, when you write, go into your room and close the door. There is a good God who takes great delight in what He's made, who knit you together in your mother's womb. And when you sing, when you write, do it for that beautiful King. Not any other.

Do it for the one who loved you when you hated Him.

Who saw you when you were hidden.

Who sits with you when everyone else has walked away.

His opinion is the one that matters. And He LOVES what He made when He fashioned YOU.

So, sing, friend.

Sing!

Holy Contemplation:
Where have you allowed the marketplace, or the opinions of others, to define
the value of your design? Of your offering? How can you return today to the
simplicity of devotion to Christ? How can you create, work, live before HIS
eyes? You were made to worship! Your giftedness is part of your offering.
Bring it to Him today!

DOORS...

There's something about an old worn door

that makes you long that it could speak

To tell you the stories of how it's opened and closed

and hidden so many mysteries.

From one side to another everything can change

atmospheres and cultures, emotions and names

what would you say if I asked you the question,

"Tell me your story?" What would you mention?

Should I knock? Should I reach for the handle to see

if it willingly yields to the wonder in me?

Should I stand and just wait?

Maybe waiting's the bait?

To provoke the latch

To change the door's state

From where I stand,

As a mother, a wife

how much could this door

change the course of my life?

Holy Contemplation:
Our lives are filled with doors. Have you ever noticed? Every day, every
year, a million little choices for change. We can look with intention...
knocking, seeking, asking, or we can react to what comes. I believe there is
an opportunity in the knocking if only we would have the courage to lift our
hand to every seemingly closed door. There is partnership in the asking. If
only we could be brave enough to lift our wobbly voices to the keeper of all
keys.

What if today, the invitation is to lift your hand to the door? What if today,
the invitation is to lift your voice to the God who hears? What if, instead of
reacting, we acted—gathering up our weary souls and charging into the
unknown? What door in your life deserves a good, solid, knock? Let's lift our
hands and our voices together. Who knows... maybe the door will open!

"And I tell you, ask, and it will be given to you; seek, and you will find;
knock, and it will be opened to you" (Luke 11:9 ESV).

WHAT'S THE POINT? ...

"Do you ever ask yourself, 'What is my purpose? Why am I here? What am I supposed to do with my life?'"

The tears were rolling down my nine-year-old daughter's cheeks as she erupted with a deep longing to understand. I sat down on the bed with trepidation. This was a holy moment, and it was clear God wanted our attention. I put my hand on her knee and waited. Restraining myself from saying a word in hopes that she would expound.

She continued to communicate that she just wants to know what her life is about. What is she meant to do? Why was she made? After a little while, she stopped talking and just waited, like she wanted me to answer her.

The whole time she was talking, I was praying, "Lord, help! Give me wisdom. Speak through me."

Finally, these words poured out...

"Your whole life is full of these little whispers, like clues, that the Lord knit inside of you while you were still in my womb. If you are paying attention, you can begin to piece the clues

together to find your design. It's sort of like
putting together a puzzle!

"What are some things that make you feel joy?
Make you feel alive? Things that, when they are
happening, you feel strength come up from your
toes, breath fill your lungs, and excitement fill
your spirit?"

She waited thoughtfully for quite a while and
then, with definition and quiet resolve, she began
to answer my slew of prompts, "Being with my
family gives me so much joy!"

The tears rolled down her cheeks.

"And riding horses makes me feel strong and
free!"

I smiled and said, "Good, those are whispers!"

"Being with my baby sister, seeing her happy,
that makes me so happy!" she continued.

Now my tears began to well up, and I whispered,
"Well, baby, that's a clue into your design!"

Then she threw herself long into my arms.

While I was holding her and rocking her, I felt a surge of fire swell in me. I knew it was an anchor in the tumult of this question that she will carry with her for the rest of her life...

"The most important thing for you to remember is that you were not an accident. YOU were designed with great delight and every fiber of who you are—God calls it GOOD! He rejoices over you every day! And if you never do another thing, you—just being you—that's enough!"

Oh, how quickly we forget this truth. In a world clamoring for MORE, screaming at us that we are endlessly falling short or running out of time... there is a good Creator, gazing at what He so masterfully knit together, and rejoicing over us!

You... beloved, like my Aidah, are cherished.

YOU are loved.

YOU are NOT an accident.

You were made with divine purpose and every fiber of your frame and breath is VERY GOOD.

Holy Contemplation:
Do you believe that, friend? That you, just being you... is enough? What are
some of the whispers of your design? What has God been writing through
you from before the foundations of time? Do you know that if you never do
another thing, His endless delight for the very good creation He knit together
would never wane? It would never falter! You can't change His mind! Do you
believe it? Placing your hand on your own heart, whisper these words with
me: "Jesus, you love what you made. I am yours and that's enough."

HOPE AGAINST HOPE...

Autumn is in the air. The changing of leaves, the turning of seasons.

Normally, we are in a hurry for the winter to pass and the spring to come. But this year, the heat of the summer has scorched us in so many ways. We find our hearts longing for the crisp, cool air of autumn.

My heart has ached in ways I have never known in this blistering season that's passing. My disappointment in the body of Christ: the lack of compassion, betrayal of self-control, the raising of political and opinionated banners so much higher than the love for and the goodness of God.

I've been blistered by a culture that seems to be more concerned with the sound of our own voices than the sound of His holy voice.

I've watched brother turn against brother, sister slander and mock sister, and pastors preach prideful opinions from their pulpits instead of the gospel of Jesus Christ.

I've heard so many, in their observations of "Christian" behavior, wonder where the character of Christ has gone. Where the fruits of His Spirit can be found. And I've personally suffered the blows of judgement and accusation from my own brothers and sisters in Christ, unlike anything I've ever known.

As someone who has felt called to and passionate about preparing the bride unto Christ's return, my ache for her current condition has cut me to the core.

For the first time in my faith, I have wrestled with
a despairing that she might not ever be ready. We
might never be prepared.

How will we reflect Him in His goodness and
glory if we can't even honor the parts that we
disagree with? How will each part work together in
submission to the head if we continue to mutilate and
cut off every part that does not yield to our personal
agendas?

BUT... I can't stop there.
We
can't
stop there.

I was speaking with a friend yesterday, and this
phrase came out of my mouth as if springing up from
the hidden places of my heart, the wells of history
and hope that do not yield to circumstances and
disappointment:

"I've been very achy and grieved over her [the bride
of Christ's] condition. But I am confident in the
goodness of God, and His ability to prepare even a
harlot to be His bride. Jesus is the only hope. Jesus is
the only answer."

We have a hope against all hopes.

We have a Savior who's mighty to save.

We have a Father who is slow to anger and
abounding in love.

We have a Creator who brings beauty from ashes
and makes harlots His bride. Who grabs beggars
from gutters and crowns them as kings. Who takes
the weakest, the most desolate, the most hopeless
of circumstances and breathes His breath of
redemption, pours His blood of atonement, offers His
body up as a sacrifice so that we... the ones He loves
despite all our faithlessness and immaturity... might
become holy as He is holy.

Without stain or wrinkle.

Without spot or blemish.

So that the harlots who have given ourselves to the
loves of selfish ambition, pride, self-gratification,
self-promotion, wealth, position, entitlement,
politics, knowledge, and title, might be washed in the
cleansing flow of HIS sacrifice and stand blameless
by His side.

I don't know how He will do it.

I can't fathom the chasm He must bridge for us to
meet Him there.

But I am confident in His ability to accomplish every
good work that He began.

I am confident that He gets the final word. That HE
is the beginning and the end. That NOTHING is too

far gone for Him.

I don't know HOW... but I know He WILL.

And while the tears pour down my cheeks, I will
set my face to the Son, and surely He will rise again
over this generation.

My hope is in God.
My hope is in HIS unfailing love.

My hope has an anchor in this violent storm... His
name is Immanuel and He is GOD WITH US.

Prayerful Meditation:
Jesus, we have nothing good apart from you.
Jesus, we can DO NOTHING without you.
Jesus, you are the King who makes wrong things right.
You are the Savior who makes harlots His bride.
May the mercy and compassion that burns in you, now burn in me.
For myself and for all humanity.
May the zeal that consumes you, consume me.
And may the JOY that was set before you, be set before me.
God, will you grant me HOPE today?
I am not my own.
Take and hold my heart again.
I am yours alone.

WHAT IS TRUTH...

Have you ever thought about standing on the shore of life or diving into the waves? How, so often, we rationalize our dreams away because deep down we don't feel adequate, or we disqualify ourselves because we've been listening to the accuser for so long?

This past Sunday, I heard one of the most profound messages on identity that I'd ever heard. In the speaker's process, she quoted this verse:

"He has always hated the truth, because there is no truth in him. When he lies, it is consistent with his character; for he is a liar, the father of lies. So, when I tell the truth you just naturally don't believe me" (John 8:44-45 NLT).

I was so struck with the reality that when we entertain the lies of inadequacy for long enough, we can actually get to a place where we aren't able to receive the truth anymore.

We are no longer able to hear it.

What if we were really created for greater works?

What if we really can do ALL things through Christ who strengthens us?

What if we really are more than conquerors?

What if we stopped listening to every voice that says, "You can't, you aren't good enough, you don't have what it takes, you'll fail miserably, everyone will laugh at you, who do you think you are...?" And instead, we let the TRUTH become our anthem...

Truth… is a person.

His name is the Living Word.

He has a voice… and He's speaking to you, even now.

I don't know about you, but I don't want to get so accustomed to the sound of the accuser of the brethren that I can't hear the truth anymore!

It's time to take every single thought captive according to the WORD of God.
To rehearse HIS truth.
To wrap it around our hearts until we STAND!
As sons and daughters.
The very sons and daughters that creation has been groaning for.

I once heard a pastor say, "In your mind, you make a decision; in due season, your heart will catch up."

So, why don't we make a decision today?

Say it with me:

"I AM
A CHILD
OF GOD."

Prayerful Meditation:
Father, I confess that I have entertained the accusations of the enemy concerning my identity. Will you please forgive me? I ask that you would come now, as the God of all TRUTH, and fill my heart and soul with the knowledge of who you say I am. Wrap your truth around me. Help me to write it on my heart and meditate on your word. May it truly be a weapon in my hand against every fiery dart of the father of lies that comes my way. Amen.

COMPASSIONATE BENDING...

I recently found myself on an "adventure" with my kiddos. I had all these grand ideas of how it was going to go.

Do you ever do that? Play it all out? Think you are giving your kids this glorious gift of goodness and then, BAM, it completely backfires and you're left holding REAL life right there in your humbled hands?

It usually goes something like this...

Our ideals for adventure or making a good memory as a family are laid out before us. We're fighting to seize the moment, and SUDDENLY it gets flooded with little hearts learning to process their emotions, big hearts learning to lead through frustration, a reach... from parent to child, struggling to connect on the root issue, to resolve the disenchanted heart and awkwardly lead them back into the goodness of the moment. All while being uncertain if you are doing it right, fighting for your own self control while attempting to TEACH self control, and ultimately spending yourself, not on the atmosphere around you, but more on the atmosphere within you and within them.

{sigh}

Sound familiar?

So much of parenting (or relationship in general) is filled with moments where we must bend down, look our children or loved ones in the eyes, listen to the roaring rush of feelings pouring from their guts... I mean REALLY listen, and then slowly, carefully,

with gentleness and compassion hanging on every
word,

lead them from the cliff of their emotions, across
the chasm of despair, over the bridge of grace, to
the refuge of truth.

It's challenging.

It can be a torrential downpour.

But I think it's what love looks like.

Laying down our best laid plans to be present
and intentional with the ones right in front of
us. Forsaking the "storybook ending" for the
compassionate bending… to meet them where they
are and lead them to higher ground. A higher way.
The Highest ONE.

We're all working out our faith, aren't we? What a
privilege to do it together.

Holy Contemplation:
Is there someone in your life right now who could use your compassionate
bending? Some circumstance where you had ideals that are falling apart, and
instead of being frustrated about the collapse of ideals, you could turn your
heart to the person in front of you and really listen? In what areas of your life
could you lead by example today by meeting someone where they are instead
of fighting for your own outcome? To leave the ninety-nine for the one (Luke
15). Who is your one?

A GOD WHO FEELS...

During the dreaded pandemic, I had a day (many days!) where my heart and mind got completely overwhelmed by the details. I thought about the condition of the world we were living in. Conspiracy theories, terrifying statistics, death toll charts, politics, and politicians. I thought about rioting and racism, police brutality and police being brutalized, children being exploited, and mothers and fathers dying alone in hospital rooms. My mind was consumed with thoughts of schools, teachers, parents, vaccines, masks, businesses, jobs, workers, and all the shouting from every part of our world exploded in my head like alarms going off, demanding my response!

Then, before I completely tangled myself into a web of opinions, I laid hold of my overwhelmed heart, and, with great intention, I turned it toward one, profoundly encompassing word ...
"Compassion."

Then the tears fell.

I let myself actually FEEL and not think.

Do you know what I found? Compassion cannot be whittled down to an analytical anecdote that we acknowledge in language but fail to respond to with a heart that feels. It requires us to shut our mouths long enough to feel another's ache.

It starts not with self—not self-preservation, not self-awareness, not self-proclamation, not the opinions or deductions I have crafted for my SELF. It starts with looking out, seeing the ache, and then refusing to rush past it with our opinions—instead, lingering,

quieting the traffic in our minds long enough to
actually weep with those who weep.

Compassion doesn't have a political party.
It doesn't care what the numbers say or if the stats
are off.

Compassion leaves the ninety-nine for the one and
then sits with them in their pain (Luke 15).

This world is FULL of pain. I keep looking for
friends of the God who embodied the very fullness
of justice and truth, and yet His first response was
often compassion.

Is it possible compassion precedes true justice?

Friend, fight for truth, but do not forsake compassion.
If we do that, we've put the cart before the horse.

1 John 4:20 says, "If anyone says, 'I love God,' and
hates his brother, he is a liar; for he who does not
love his brother whom he has seen cannot love God
whom he has not seen" (ESV).

It's time to cultivate compassion.

Prayerful Meditation:
God of compassion, you who are slow to anger and abounding in great
love, will you teach me your way today? You are meek. Help me be meek.
When you, God, see the world raging, what do you feel? You are a God with
emotions, and I was made in your image. So, as you feel today, will you share
it with me? Can I feel WITH you? I want to be your friend. I want my heart to
be moved with compassion.

WILLING TO DIE...

I can hear my mama's words on repeat in my head these days:

"Two wrongs don't make a right! You can't fight fire with fire."

Isn't it amazing how what felt like a childhood broken record grows into the sweetest kind of wisdom? It's simple, right?! So simple, that I think we easily forget and wander out of bounds.

In Luke 6:27-28, Jesus says it like this:
"But I say to you who hear, love your enemies, do good to those who hate you, bless those who curse you, pray for those who abuse you" (ESV).

It takes real discipline to turn the other cheek! Tenacity, to use our tongues for blessing when we've just been cursed. Endurance, to remain quiet when slander abounds. Resilience, to genuinely pray for the very people who have hate in their hearts and gossip on their tongues against you or someone you love.

I'm 41 years old, and I'm still baffled by the way of the Kingdom.
The WAY of my King.

I'm undone by the meekness of Christ.
Awestruck by His silence to the cross and His ability to stay the course when a world of slander and false accusation raged against Him.

I was reading in Acts the other day, and there was

this one little line about the apostles: They went
away rejoicing to be counted worthy to suffer for the
gospel (Acts 5:41, my own paraphrase).

REJOICING?

For SUFFERING?

I don't know if I'll ever quite get my knee jerk
reactions to life and injustice to respond like Christ's,
but I sure aim to try. To lean in a little harder, to go a
little lower, to bite my tongue a little longer, to bless
in the face of cursing, to pray for those who abuse
me, to do good to those who hate me...

to simply refuse... to fight fire with fire.

We might not ever be master's friend.
We might still be a long way off.
But even when the son was "Still a long way off" his
father came running to meet him!

The Father is running to meet you.

Holy Contemplation:
Is there a circumstance or a person in your life right now in which you have
been tempted to fight fire with fire? How might the Lord lead your heart
into His way? What if, instead of ruminating over the injustice, you began
to pray for the one who is perpetrating that injustice against you? Begin to
bless them with your prayers, with your mouth. Watch and see if He doesn't
strengthen and soften your heart in the process. His ways aren't naturally
our ways. But He really loves to show us the way!

LOWER STILL...

"So... it's like, it's backwards?"
These were the words that came spilling out of my curious, eight-year-old son the other night. Sibling rivalry had taken hold of his afternoon, and it was time for bed, but I wanted to make sure his heart was clean and free before he shut his eyes.

"Did you clean up your mess with your sister?" I asked. ("Clean up your mess" is a phrase we use when we make a relational mistake or step out of bounds in our house.) He quickly jumped to his own defense. Every reason why he was justified in his behavior came pouring out of his mouth. I must say, he put forth a solid case. "Hmmm... but what could YOU have done differently in that situation?" I asked him gently. Quietness followed by a meek, mumbled sentence: "Probably... a lot of things." he said.

"Buddy, did you know that the Bible says that the last shall be first? It says that if you humble yourself, the Lord will exalt you. It also says that we shouldn't do anything from selfish ambition, but instead, we should count others more significant than ourselves. Even when we have a bunch of good reasons why we feel justified, we can go lower still. If we do that, Jesus promises to lift us up."

Tears began to well up in his eyes as he let the
words soak all the way in. Then, without another
word from me, he said it.

"So... it's like, it's backwards?"
Yeah! It's kind of like it's backwards! His
ways aren't our ways. His thoughts aren't our
thoughts. They're better! They're higher! In
order to get on His level, to walk in His way,
we've got to go lower still.

Teaching my children has been one of my
greatest teachers. Even as I spoke to him, I could
feel my heart beginning to bend before the Lord.
So many more places I could go lower still.

He jumped up, not a moment to spare, and went
to his sister. He bent low, and the fragrance of
that humbled heart reaching for God's kingdom
was enough to provoke this mama to do the
same.

Holy Contemplation:
Where can you go lower still? Where can you bow your heart just a little
further on this journey of making room for His kingdom to come? Maybe it's
time for us to live a little backwards from what the world says is the right
way. As you move through your day today, watch for ways to bend. To take
the last place. To lean into the humility and meekness of your Maker. You just
might find that what you do in secret, He'll reward openly. He's closer than
you think.

WIN

T E R

SLOW + SACRED

"Reframe the way you see this season of winter. Recast the struggle for what it is, an opportunity for God to do again what He does best: flip a story on its head and resurrect life out of death."

Max Lucado

"Like the cold snow in the time of harvest is a faithful messenger to those who send him, for he refreshes the soul of his masters."

Proverbs 25:13 (NASB)

WINTER

It's quiet now

Everything has gone to sleep

Buried under ice and snow, freezing temperatures make
breathing slow

"SURVIVE!" is the groan of the living things

And death is the invitation that winter brings

Not time to build

Not time to grow

Time to surrender to the whispering unknown

To steady our rhythms

To slumber and sleep

To rest and not fight the bitter, cold quieting

Have you ever heard it?

That draping blanket of snow

It's as if the whole world has been muted and knows…

Winter is for restoring the soul

AVAILABLE …

It was 11:30 p.m. We were all tired and thin. The kind of exhausted that feels as though it's tearing through your insides slowly and pulling out all sense of stability and strength. We'd been burning the candle at both ends for months. The moving truck was arriving in the morning to change the course of our lives forever, and I was NOT ready.

I was looking at my house in its wreckage, navigating my heart in its own wreckage, and listening to my baby cry incessantly, refusing to be comforted. Resisting sleep like it was a poison. All my tried-and-true mom tactics were failing, and the exasperation was overwhelming my whole frame.

You know those moments that almost feel like time stands still for half a second? It's like everything freezes. There's a divine pause as though someone slowed the reel of your life down just enough for you to catch what's really unfolding around you.

That's when I heard it… that still, small voice whisper—that everlasting, perfect counsel—and suddenly I felt like the solution had been obvious the whole time.

"Just stop. Just hold him."

And so, turning aside from every unpacked box and time-sensitive demand, I reached down into that crib, scooped that tiny frame up into my trembling arms, walked slowly to the rocking chair in the corner of the room, inhaled a broken breath, exhaled with tears brimming over my eyelids, and stopped.

Moments later, he was fast asleep on my shoulder.

You know what I realized in that holy, slow-motion moment? That still, small voice comes from a Father: a Father who's never too busy, overwhelmed, or stressed out to know just what to do with my tired, overstimulated, overextended, broken-hearted self. He stops everything so I can rest. On His shoulder. Listening to His heartbeat. Finding my comfort and my peace in His arms.

He is the Ever-Present God. The Everlasting Father. The Prince of Peace. His arms do not get tired. His awareness and availability are never eclipsed by clamoring circumstances. Omnipresent.

He's ALWAYS PRESENT.

We live in a time in which presence is one of the most rare and precious currencies. Humanity's lack of presence communicates to our broken hearts that there isn't time for our pain. There isn't enough space for our ache.

That our questions are too much,
that our need is too great,
and no one is available to hold our exasperated
frames.

But hear me... It just isn't true.
He is AVAILABLE to me... and to you.

The truth of that moment rooted itself in my weary
soul. If I can stop for my baby, then God most
definitely will stop for me. And that is just where I
intend to be.
Leaning on those everlasting arms.
Until my tired, broken heart surrenders into holy
sleep.

So right now, go ahead and cry out.

Go ahead and tell Him that you can't find your rest.
That you're overextended and overstimulated and
you NEED Him to be your safe place.

Go ahead and tell Him you need the PRESENT God.

Take a breath, close your eyes, find Him waiting.
Arms reaching, heart peacefully beating, compassion
brimming.

He is the Available God.

Prayerful Meditation:
Father, I need you! I'm tired and overwhelmed. I know that you are close
to the brokenhearted. Will you come close to me now? Will you let me hear
your heartbeat? Will you let me feel your wrap-around presence? I need to
feel your nearness. I need you to hold me together until the safety of your
embrace leads my heart into holy rest.

HIDDEN IN THE SNOW...

Several years ago, in a fit of mom fury and a desperate attempt to redeem any semblance of a school day, I threw the kids into the car (ok, I didn't THROW them... I buckled them) and started driving up the mountain by our house. No clear destination in mind... just desperate to change the scenery.

I remember approaching a little turn off on the side of the road, not clearly seen, but almost whispering to my wondering heart to come closer. I suddenly turned the car off the main road and drove until I couldn't drive anymore.

"Ok! Let's go see what we can see!" I announced to the cranky kiddos in the back seat.

Everyone scrambled out of the car a bit begrudgingly because we didn't know what was waiting for us around the bend. If we had known, there would have been zero delay.

Around a corner of rocks and stubble, opened a sanctuary of towering oak trees, moss-covered rock formations, ferns springing up from the ground, and the golden leaves of autumn chattering in the wind. It was magic!
Like we had stepped into a foreign land filled with the kind of wonder that makes your insides simultaneously reverberate with excitement and slow down to finally breathe.

The kids dubbed this little slice of heaven, "our secret place," and they couldn't wait to show their

182

daddy what they'd been waiting all winter to share.

You see, in the wintertime there are huge gates that close off the road that leads us to this sanctuary. So, we were all thrilled to find the gates open, declaring that the winter had passed and revealing a bubbling brook of snowmelt rushing right through the middle of this already-wonder-filled retreat.

Our secret place had taken on new life—life we didn't know it was capable of—because we only had the experience of the past season to view it through.

Our secret place was even better than before!

And isn't that the truth? The way it all works out. Winter HAS to come so certain things can die. Then all the cold bitterness must melt... so all the twinkling, exhilarating life can begin to flow again.

I don't always love the winter. But I almost always love what the winter hides for us... to be found only when we have lingered in the space where bitter cold melts away and reveals the treasures cultivated from that season.

Holy Contemplation:
Maybe you have been in a cold winter season... Hear me when I say, God has hidden treasure for you in it. I think maybe it's time for some snow to melt. For the fire of love to transform that frozen heart into something beautiful. Life has been hidden in your winter. Love and forgiveness will bring it forth.

BEAUTY FOR ASHES...

On a beautiful day in California, driving from the south to the north on a long road trip with my family, I was suddenly struck by the contrast between death and life. The last time I remembered driving through these hills, they were literally on fire. It looked like devastation everywhere, and I felt an ache in my heart as I watched the flames consume every drop of life on either side of the highway.

Then, after only a little time passed, those same scorched and barren hills were springing forth with new life! A stunning display of floral colors rested delicately upon their shoulders. While taking in this beautiful reflection of His majesty, holding hands with my best friend, I began thinking about the fight through the ashes that marriage can and often times has been.

Human beings can be messy creatures, can't we?

Then, when you put us together in close quarters for years on end, our mess can get all over each other. At times it can even look like devastation is sweeping across the landscape of our hearts. But here's the beauty of a love that bears all things, believes all things, dares to hope all things, and, with both hands clinging to a promise, says, "I will suffer long with you."

That kind of love, which only comes from the source of Love itself and with the help of Love itself...
that kind of love pushes through ashes and devastation and says,
"I'm still here! I was under the surface of immaturity, weakness, insecurity, and pain, but now I'm bursting with fresh beauty, color, and life!"

Maybe for you, in this season of your life, all you can
see is devastation sweeping across the landscape of
your heart? Your relationships might look like fire
is consuming them, or the fire came and went and
there's nothing visible but a sea of ash.

I say to you today...
hold on.

Cling to the source of love with both hands and, with
His sweet help, declare,
"I will suffer long with you. I will dare to hope all
things. I will bear up under this ash heap until the
promises we whispered and those whispered to us,
spring forth with fresh life and vibrant color across
the landscape of our hearts."

The winter will pass, and the springtime will come.
And joy really does come in the morning.
Just hold on, friend.

Because the God I know—He exchanges beauty for
ashes. And if all you see are ashes... then He's not
finished yet.

Prayerful Meditation:
Beautiful creator God, the one who takes the ash heaps of our lives and
blows His breath of love over them until the beauty arises, today... in
my going out and in my coming in, in my aching and my longing, in my
weariness and doubt... I hold up these ashes and beckon you to take them!
And in the waiting... I will trust that you have hidden color, promise,
fragrance, hope, healing, and new life in the soil of this heart of mine. I trust
you to bring it forth from my little life. I trust you to make the landscape of
my scorched heart bloom again. Help me trust you more today. Amen.

GRIEF + GRATITUDE...

It seems to me that life is full of moments where deep gratitude is tangled up with groaning ache. How so often we experience both and desperately try to untangle the two. But I don't think we were meant to untangle them at all. Somehow the ache makes room for the gratitude. And the gratitude? Well, it digs down deeper in the wake of ache.

It was on a Friday that our family, with deep gratitude in our hearts, celebrated the gift of life growing inside my womb. The following Wednesday, at nine weeks, we became overwhelmed with the flooding ache of that baby joining our other two babies in heaven.

The deep swell of gratitude remained
present with the pain.
Because LIFE is always a gift.
Every season, every stage, for a
moment, or for eighty years... LIFE is
worth celebrating.
Acknowledging.
Raising our voice and our song for.
I don't know if there is another gift
more precious, more valuable, more
costly...
than LIFE.

To this day, my longing for our baby
has not dissipated, and yet my eternity
holds promise and hope. I live in the
tension. We all live in the tension.
I think the invitation is in who we
welcome into that tension with us. We
weren't meant to hold it alone.

Prayerful Meditation:
Giver of Life, you give the greatest gifts. Man of Sorrows, you know my
deepest ache. I won't try to untangle the two. I will just sit here and hold them
both... with you.

LOVING US THROUGH...

My remarkably patient husband, Ryan, gets all my
unfiltered, raw, and rowdy process.
And let's be honest, there's a LOT!
What overwhelms my heart, though, is that he
almost never flinches. Somehow he knows I'm going
to come around that rowdy mountain. He knows I'll
land somewhere between repentance and clinging
harder to Jesus.
And he loves me not because he knows I'll get there,
but he loves me... ALL THE WAY THERE.
Every peak, every plummet, every weary step.
Because love leads. Love covers. Love always wins.

We will have been married for twenty years this
March, and as I look back on every year, the wisdom
and kindness of God astound me. There are a million
details about this man that I never knew I always
needed (and a few that drive me crazy, and a ton that
I adore),
but the Lord knew.

And we haven't always gotten it right, but we have
learned to love each other THROUGH, not despite.

To stare the gnarly, ugly junk in the face, not shrink
back from it, AND keep moving
forward,
upward,
onward. (Sometimes downward... as in, on our faces
in prayer.)

I think we often expect the ones we love to
eventually arrive at our ideal destination of character
wholeness. But I'm learning that when Jesus

promised us that love was slow to anger, when Paul
reminded us that love suffers long and it keeps no
record of wrong, it was because that's the kind of
love humanity REQUIRES.

We don't always get it right, do we?
We aren't as good at loving like the source of love
Himself.

But after twenty-plus years of marriage, I'm
more certain that Jesus is the King who loves us
THROUGH.
Not when.
Not because of.
But all the way THROUGH.
Until the reward of His suffering is standing before
Him as a suitable counterpart. Reflecting HIM in all
of HIS glory.

Because His love... that perfect, patient, long
suffering kind of love... it doesn't love us despite our
mess, it loves us THROUGH it.

Holy Contemplation:
How can you let Him love you today? How might you trust the journey of love
more truly than the destination of it? His love is enough to carry us through.
Whisper with me these words:
"I'm going to let you love me."

"And now these three remain: faith, hope and love. But the greatest of these is
LOVE" (1 Corinthians 13:13 NIV, emphasis added).

AT THE END OF MYSELF...

When I was a little girl, somewhere close to the age of nine or ten, a glorious snow had blanketed the whole southern region where we lived. Snow was common every winter, but not THIS MUCH snow.

Naturally, all the schools sent out the delightful news that classes had been canceled for the day. Permission to turn our front yard blanket of white glory into our very own playground was enthusiastically received! I recruited my older brother (he must have been twelve or thirteen at the time) to help me build the most epic snowman we could manage. After rolling the first giant ball of grass-filled snow around the yard and securing it into place with big icy globs around the base, my brother went in for a snack break.

I've always been the type of person who, once I have vision for something and start it, I want to push it through to the end with all my might. So naturally, I wasn't ready for a break because the epic snow man wasn't finished yet. I decided, in my determination, that I would just roll and place the second ball myself.
"Who needs him?" I thought.

The problem was that the size of the ball and the size of my slight nine-year-old frame were in direct competition. By the time I got the ball to the base

and began to attempt to lift it by forcing every fiber
of my being against the weight pressing back on
me, I quickly realized that I was no match for this
giant snow belly. The problem was, I already had it
suspended in the air, wedged between its base and
my body, and I was STUCK!

I began to scream for my brother. A desperate kind
of scream. When you are using all your strength to
hold things together and your failure is taunting you
in the face.

I was MAD!

Mad that I didn't have the strength to do it myself.
Mad that my brother didn't mirror my enthusiasm.
Mad that I'd gotten myself into this ridiculous snow
pickle.

The only way out now was helping hands or
complete destruction of my dream. And then it
happened: the pressure of the snow belly and all my
body weight forcing against it suspended halfway up
the base, caused the base to break!
SNAP!
All my epic snow dreams sent me falling to the
ground with a crumble of snowman around me.

I began to sob! A deep and devastated sob. It was
only then that my brother, Nathan, came out to find
me weeping in the snow with the remains of what we
had spent the morning building together in shambles
all around me.

"What happened? Why are you crying?" he said in a sort of annoyed, yet genuinely concerned, way. Through my sobs I accused him of not being there! Not helping me when I needed him most. His reply cut me to the core...

"All you had to do was wait. If you would have waited... none of this would have happened."

"Apart from me, you can do nothing" (John 15:5 NIV).
It's like we all read that verse and just skim over it, then pull up our imaginary human bootstraps and take matters into our own hands.

I don't think it's simply the head knowledge or even the verbal agreement with dependence that we, as humans, need to make. I THINK we actually have to be emptied of our own ability sometimes in order to set things in proper order.
Literally coming to the end of ourselves and then admitting, without apology, we need help!

That kind of emptying—it's not glamorous.
It's not being trumpeted from very many platforms. But that kind of emptying—that's the kind of weakness I think Paul was saying he could boast in. Not because it was boast-worthy, but because he understood that when we get there, God's REAL power is made perfect in THAT place!

Why are we so afraid of the end of ourselves?

What do we think will happen when we arrive at that

intimidating destination?

How quickly we forget that we were not designed to
be independent, but dependent!

There is no shame in our desperate need for a Savior!

There is no shame in clinging to a rock that is higher.

There is NO shame in leaning our weary bodies into
the strength of His might.

So today, I say to you, "Shame off you!"
Go ahead and lean, unapologetically.
Fall desperately and completely into those
everlasting arms.
Laugh at the chaos.
Linger in the hug.
And know that you are perfectly safe at the end of
yourself because He is more than enough.

Holy Contemplation:
What areas in your life are screaming under the pressure of trying to do it
yourself? What snowballs have you wedged between your own strength and
your desperate need for the Helper? Where in your life, today, could you
"wait on the Lord" instead of charging ahead without Him? His arms are
available to you. If you feel like you are at the end of yourself, maybe it's time
to fall into Him.

HE CAN DO A LOT WITH ONE STEP...

In the gospels, we see Jesus take His leave
of the crowds. It was His custom to go away
to a quiet place to talk to His Father. But
today, we go away to a quiet place and bring
our phones, which are far from quiet. It
seems more and more difficult to find a still
space in our current day and age.

Yesterday, I NEEDED a quiet place with my
Father. For a home school mama, that means
I must get creative. So up to the mountains
we went. Audiobook in my children's ears
while I drove, I began the conversation
with God. Then, finding a quiet place by
the stream and setting them to their tasks, I
listened for the voice of my Father.

What still takes my breath away, even after
knowing and loving Jesus for over twenty-
five years, is that whatever I have to give
Him... no matter how weak, small, broken,
dirty, or messy it is... as soon as I take that
first step, He meets me.

You see, He's not a father who makes us
jump through hoops or climb some ladder
just to be where He is. No, friend, He's the

kind of Father who, when we've screwed it
all up,
when our hearts are a big, muddy mess,
when we are still a LONG. WAY. OFF.—
that's when He RUNS to meet us.

I needed to remember this yesterday, as my
heart was spilling everywhere.
And I need to remember it every day, as I
fight my way through all the noise.

Sometimes we let the culture of this age
define for us the character of our Father. We
let men and women—who are just as broken
as we are—become His definition. And this
subtle ache or lack of trust starts to creep
into our hearts.

We start performing, keeping up with
the Joneses, thinking God has some
uncommunicated expectation of us, and our
inability to discern it means we will surely
fail. We fear He will turn His back on us in
disappointment or dissatisfaction and, with
a new agenda, pick the next person in line.

But HE is NOT the culture of this age.
His love is NOT conditional or fickle.
He doesn't use or abuse us for His own
personal gain.
He doesn't forget His commitments, and He
is ALWAYS available.

Sometimes we need to strengthen ourselves
in the Lord, but sometimes, when we've got
nothing left, we just need to take one step.

It's ok if all you have in you right now is one
step.

I know a Shepherd who leaves the ninety-
nine for the one.
I know a Father who runs to meet you when
you are still a long way off.
I know a King who crowns beggars and
a Prince who shares the wealth of His
inheritance with the poor and needy.
That King,
that Father,
that Prince… He's available today.
One step… He can do a lot with one step.

Prayerful Meditation:
Father, I feel like I'm a long way off. You feel far and I feel tired, disqualified,
and weak. I intentionally turn my heart towards you today. I take the first
step in returning to your presence. Will you run to meet me? Please God,
come and meet me. Amen.

GOD WITH US...

Every year, in the four to five weeks preceding
Christmas, we go on a journey as a family through
a beautiful advent study written by a stunning home
school mama who has since gone to be with Jesus.

Every year, we are drawn deeper into the Christ of
Christmas. Drawn OUT of the hustle and bustle to a
slower rhythm of beholding God.
Of expecting God.

This year, we are finding great grace on our journey.
Maybe it's the fact that our kids are a year older,
so the conversations are deeper? Or maybe it's
because I'm growing this baby in my womb, and
the limitations are real? Either way, I feel like I'm
discovering the holy expectation that comes with
watching and waiting for something so good.

I think, in our modern-day western culture, our lack
of "need" can squelch our expectation. This year,
though, I feel so deeply acquainted with how much I
NEED Him to be the Jesus of the Christmas story.

I need Him to come.

I need Him to be Immanuel, God with me.
Not just the language of that. Not the fluffy, Sunday-
morning reality of that. Not the corporate gathering,
big platform, fleshy-networking-muddy-mess we
sometimes call "Christianity" here in the west. But
the soul gripping, heart wrenching, deep desperation
for a God who doesn't just HEAR and SEE and
KNOW, but CARES and COMES to those who call
upon His name!

THAT's the Christ of Christmas. God with us. Right here in all the "stuff" WITH us. That's where my expectation lies. That's what I ache for when I lay my head to rest at night.

Oh, how I need Him to be THAT God. The one we don't have to qualify for, but instead, when we can't get it "right," He humbles himself down to the dust and comes to be WITH us.
To walk alongside.
To lead in the flesh.
The help. To hold. To cry with. To touch. To feel.
To be present.

Because of who HE IS. Not because of what we've done or haven't done. Because of HIS great love. Not because we are able to love Him rightly. The God who doesn't leave us or forsake us. The God who fights for us when we don't recognize the fight in our own hearts.

The God who crosses the chasm of the cosmos, bends down to the dust from which we were made, and whispers...
"You're the one I want.
You are worth my fight.
My love for you cannot be stopped or thwarted... not even by you.
Here I AM! HERE, beloved... WITH YOU."

That's the God I need. That's the CHRIST of Christmas.

Prayerful Meditation:
Immanuel, God with me, I confess to you my deep and aching need for your nearness. For your humanity to collide with my humanity. For your divinity to override every impossibility. I need you to be the Christ of Christmas today. Break into my weary world with HOPE and rejoicing. Interrupt my mundane work with holy visitation. Humble every lofty ambition with the meekness of your ways. Be Immanuel... Be God WITH me today. Amen today."

LAMENT...

Tired heart
Tired heart
Don't give up
Don't give up
There's a song that's been locked in your soul

Every weight that you bare
Every tear that you've shared
It whispers the way to your home

Time, it takes its toll
When you find all that hides in the shadows
But you have a choice to make
Will you bend in your ache
Or break

Hope is not hope at all
If you think that your eyes should behold it
A promise, it grows in the locked grip of those
Who refuse, I refuse to let go

Tired heart
Tired heart
Don't give up
Don't give up
On that song that's been torn through your soul

LOOKING FOR HOPE...

I'm digging down deep for hope today.

HOPE... it's such a complex word. It has so many different facets and twists and turns. As I unpack this ancient trunk of life, filled with centuries of oddities that could look like they have no relation to each other, I am confronted with an invitation.

This fragile assembly of blood and bone— humanity as we know it—can take each piece we pull from this trunk and view it as a random scrap...
or with hearts pounding with anticipation, and, minds racing with expectation, we can reconcile that there is a bigger picture of something GOOD woven through these scraps.
Something full of promise.
Something full of HOPE.
There is something bigger than our random, odd little lives.
And THAT something bigger makes each piece in the trunk significant.

The invitation is to see, through every season of question, that there is a divine

story being written and that everything
that has breath is not just a disposable
afterthought, but an integral part of a
complete thought.

A divine thought.

A thought that is filled with goodness
beyond comprehension. Wrapped in a
relentless love. Driven by a passionate
pursuit.
A thought that is a dream, ever unfolding.
A holy dream. A good, patient, Father's
dream.

If we can remember that—if we can keep
it in our minds and hearts as we examine
every odd event, every thread of life that
has woven this complex tapestry—we might
just stumble right into HOPE.

Holy Contemplation:
You, dear one, are not an afterthought.
Your story is, not an insignificant cog in a massive machine.
You, beloved, are a divine, glorious, magnificent dream.
Your life is part of a fascinating story that started with a love that knows no end.
No piece unrelated. No moment unimportant. No breath or tear or laugh wasted.
Come, now, we are not those who shrink back and are destroyed.
Come, friend, let us stumble into hope... together.

SCRAPED KNEES...

Today, my youngest daughter had a huge tumble on concrete and gravel. She ripped open both knees and an elbow. The screaming that followed was long, loud, and hysterical. She's never been that upset before.

After cleaning her wounds, stopping the bleeding, applying pressure (in the form of a bear hug) to her little body to try to calm her, anointing her tiny feet with essential oils, and even trying to bribe her with Starburst candy (that's a big deal in our house), I was completely failing at settling her sweet, fragile frame.

Insert: daddy to the rescue.

I'm pretty sure what took me an hour, took him ten minutes. She fell asleep on his chest, and then he brought her back to lay down so she could really rest. And even though he had 300 things to do... he stayed.

The truth is that my heart feels a little like
her knees lately. Can you relate? I think, if I
were two years old, I might just give myself
permission to be a little hysterical for over
an hour. But when I watched this moment
unfold, it reminded my soul where to go
with all my scrapes and wounds.

The Father. He's the safest, most constant,
most comforting, and most compassionate
One I know.
Peace reigns in His embrace.
He isn't fickle.
And He never changes.
He's not impatient, and He doesn't seek His
own.
He sees the big picture and knows how to
lead our hearts through the pain.

He holds us till we can breathe.
He holds us till we can sleep.
He holds us... and carries us into perfect
peace.

Prayerful Meditation:
Our Father. Our good, good Father. Will you keep us in perfect peace today?
Steady our minds and our bodies on you. You... and you alone.

THE TABLE OF MYSTERY...

My hero of a friend, Jan, died this week.
Suddenly. Without warning.
My heart has become a flood, and there are no gates
in the world that can hold it back from bursting.

Last night, we worshiped Jesus on the porch just like
my friend Jan would have wanted. We remembered
His sacrifice on the cross, His body broken, His
blood spilled. We gave Him our grieving hearts and
the honor we know He deserves.

There are so many questions that I have to leave on
that table of mystery.
There is not a trite answer or a bandage phrase that
any human can offer to attempt to quell what can
only be reconciled by the Divine.
But I can leave those questions right there on that
table and lift my hands up in surrender and praise.
I can let the tears pour down my cheeks in sorrow
AND adoration at the same time.

The Father can take our mingled tears and sort
them as needed, and all the swirl of ache and honor,
sorrow and celebration, unanswered questions and
faith...

they can all sit right there on that mystery table
together.

In the days and months to come, we will continue
to fill that table with more of the mingled process of
life. And then, we will do the next right thing.

I don't know a whole lot, but I DO know that love
wins.
At the end of it all, love—the perfect, relentless,
unending, patient God named Love—becomes
greater than everything else on that mystery table.

So I'll start now.
Letting Him be greater.
Lifting my hands higher.
Singing with all my guts through the grief and the
pain.

I will feast on His presence with the enemy of death
and disappointment sitting right there to watch.

Because death never gets the final word. Not when
Jesus is at the table.

Holy Contemplation:
What is the enemy at your table today? Jesus prepares a table with a feast of
His presence right in the middle of whatever enemy your soul is facing. What
would it look like for you to sit down at that table today? What would it look
like for you to PRAISE in the face of pain? God wants to make a trade. A
garment of praise for a spirit of heaviness. The choice is yours.

THE SUBSTANCE OF LOVE...

I have a friend who taught me some of the most valuable lessons of motherhood, long before I was ever a mother. She also taught me what loving someone THROUGH their pain looks like. I used to sit in her living room, sometimes until three or four in the morning, as a broken seventeen-year-old. She was mothering toddlers; I was wrestling through injustice, anger, and big life messes no human being can make sense of.

She cried with me,
laughed with me,
sat silent with me,
and shared her table and her family with me.

I will probably never know just how many prayers she prayed for me.

Her life became tangible gospel.
And it changed me.
It marked me.

I'm watching her now, twenty years later, pour her heart into MY baby girl with the same intention she poured her heart into me! It provokes me, more than ever, to live a life that truly reflects the gospel.

Living tangible gospel doesn't mean we have all the answers!
It doesn't mean we can always make the wrong things right.

But it DOES mean we can invite broken hearts into our living rooms, inconvenience our schedules, share food we aren't sure we even have enough of for our own families, look

people in the eyes, listen to their hearts, and love
them THROUGH their pain.

Jesus sat with prostitutes, drunks, and the most
broken of society.
He broke bread with them.
He let them into his life.
And it changed them.

I'm so thankful to my friend, Karen, for being a
gospel I could see, hear, and sometimes yell at
until four in the morning while I was working
it out. One of the resounding reasons my babies
know Jesus today... is because she showed Him
to me.

Our lives MUST have substance, friend.

More than language, more than Sundays, more
than shallow agreement with a "good word" or
hyping ourselves over another "movement."

The rubber meets the road when we let people
into our lives! When we LIVE Jesus in front of
their eyes.

As for me, I've still got a lot of room to grow.

Holy Contemplation:
What would tangible gospel look like in your life today? Who, on the fringes
of your world, need to see love lived before their eyes? What would it look
like to invite them to your table? To make space for their hearts and their
wrestle? Whether you feel like it or not, friend, you have something that
someone else needs. Let's embody tangible gospel today.

A TREE OF LIFE...

"Hope deferred makes the heart sick, but a desire fulfilled is a tree of life" (Proverbs 13:12 ESV).

We—like you, I'm sure—have had our share of "hope deferred" moments in the last few years. And we were reminded tonight by a friend who came over just to fight for our hearts, that we could shift our focus from "hope deferred" to "desires fulfilled."

All our journeys have these seasons where our hearts are fainting, where we don't understand, but somewhere... deep down... there is this promise of what comes when the dream or the desire is fulfilled: A TREE OF LIFE!

The truth is that hope deferred is so real, friend. It's not to be downplayed or invalidated in our ache. BUT... if our focus stays there—on the disappointment and disillusionment—then eventually, we get sick.

We have another option!
To FIGHT to find the desires fulfilled.
There are a million of those little and big victories IF we go hunting for them. And when we find them, magnify them, express our gratitude for them... do you know what happens?
Life happens! The bursting forth, the breathing in, the newness and goodness of fruitful LIFE happens.

I don't want to have a sick heart. I want to have a healthy heart. A dreaming, hoping heart.

I think that's why the second part of that verse is there.
To remind us to keep dreaming.
To keep hoping.

213

That even when our hearts are fainting... we don't have to stay there.
In fact, if we stay there, if we let that be the end of the story... we bankrupt a whole community of people who could have been nourished by the very tree of life we gave up dreaming about and fighting for.

I don't think the tree of life part was only meant for our own nourishment! If it's a tree of LIFE, to me, that means it will nourish many.

Maybe you have been barely gasping for breath under the weight of some serious hope deferred circumstances? Let's go hunting together. Let's find those desires fulfilled! And let's wrap our hearts around them until we start to see that little sprout of a tree...
Then, let's pour the water of thankfulness and remembrance all over that little sprout until it grows into a mighty oak.

Because your portion is NOT a sick heart.
Your portion is a towering, healthy, tree of LIFE!

Friend, there IS a tree of life waiting on the other side of the hopeless, heartbreaking, heartsick season you may be in.
We can't let the ache be the end of the story!
It's not the end of the verse!

"I remain confident of this: I will see the goodness of the Lord in the land of the living. Wait for the Lord; be strong and take heart and wait for the Lord." (Psalm 27:13-14 NIV).

Prayerful Meditation:
Abba, can I start with a confession? I'm disappointed! I dared to hope,
and my hopes got dashed. I'm standing here, trying to believe you for the
second part of that verse. I need your help, Jesus. I need fresh grace to
anoint my heart. I need you to help me remember the moments where I was
left holding a desire fulfilled. I turn my ache into a song of praise today. I
WILL remember your faithfulness. I WILL hold fast to your promise. I WILL
meditate on your goodness and your great deeds. This is not the end of my
story. Because this isn't the end of the verse.

STORMS...

The rain is shedding in sheets today.
The hail keeps pelting the ground and our roof
like machine guns unleashed all around us.
The thunder rumbles our bones, and the
lightning electrifies the skies.
The waters outside continue to rise.

But here, in our little home, I hold my wee
toddler in my arms, and she simply watches in
wonder. She's never seen or heard a storm like
this.
And yet... no fear.
No insecurity.
No doubt.

Her safety is found in the steadiness of my
breath,
the comfort of my embrace,
and the confidence in the sound of my voice.

She keeps looking at the storm and then looking
in my eyes.
My posture communicates to her of the
unknown.
My position becomes her position.
She is at rest because I am at rest.

And so it is with our Creator. If we look at Him
instead of the storm,
He will tell us how to respond.
He will tell us our position.
His breath, His comfort, His confidence become
our own...

IF we look to HIM instead of the storm.

216

Holy Contemplation:
Where are your eyes today? Come, let us set them on the Author and the
Finisher of our faith. Let us lift our eyes to the Beginning and the End, the
One who holds the stars and calms the storms with His hands.

What if, instead of looking at the storm, you lean in? Listen to His breath.
Look into His eyes. Rise to heavenly places and sit with Him above it all. Get
HIS perspective. Let His position become your position. There's peace to be
found in your storm.
HE is our peace in the storm.

SIMPLE OBEDIENCE...

"Well, this is new..."

Have you ever said that? I'm not one of those people who dislikes change. I actually kind of enjoy it! BUT right now, in our lives, there's so much of it that it can be difficult. When everything is new, it can feel like you don't have your footing. It's VULNERABLE!

The thing about vulnerability, though, at least from my experience, is that when you walk it all the way through, it grows into great strength. As disconcerting as it may feel, some of life's most strategic moments are born through vulnerability.

I think the key is obedience.

Regardless of how vulnerable that obedience makes you feel, regardless of how unfamiliar the territory or how inadequate the sensation in the wake of change, if your heart is set to listen and obey, every day, you will find the strength to teeter and totter through the territory of uncertainty.

Because one thing will still be certain: there is a GOOD Shepherd. He is for you and not against you. He is a perfect leader. And His sheep KNOW His voice.

So, instead of trying to figure out all the detailed "hows" of this vulnerable season I am currently finding quite new, I just keep returning to the sound of His voice.

Reminding my heart that its only responsibility is to listen… and obey.

As a mama, when my kiddos choose to trust my voice and obey my instruction, oh my goodness, that moves my heart on so many levels!

It tells me they know I'm for them.
It tells me they respect my insight or experience.
And it tells me they trust my leadership in their life... that I have their hearts.

I want Jesus to know He has my heart. That He's proven His faithfulness, and I trust Him.

And so, I return... again... to simple obedience.
It is the grace that carries this heart of mine (and yours, if you let it) through every uncertain and vulnerable season.

Prayerful Meditation:
Jesus, you have my heart. Even when everything feels vulnerable and insecure, help me incline my ear to your voice. Give me the courage to obey quickly. Grant me the grace to follow you wherever you lead. I put my trust in you today.

FIND ME LEANING...

Several years ago, our goddaughter crossed over into eternity in a very sudden and tragic way at only three years old. Ryan and I prayed and contended for her resurrection, and eventually we released her into the Father's arms. Shortly after, we suffered two consecutive and extremely painful miscarriages. To say that I slipped into a dark and confusing place is an understatement.

Out of the blue one day, a friend of mine texted me to say that Living Room Sessions (a prophetic flow album we had released shortly after these tragedies transpired) was the soundtrack of the hour. She was referencing the sweet swell of hearts that had rallied across the globe, contending for a baby girl named Olive to "wake up." Immediately, the flood of emotions from that season came rushing in.

Here's the thing: we can believe things ABOUT God, or we can expect God.
There's a difference.

When we contended for resurrection several years ago, we expected God.
When we fought for my body to hold on to our babies, we expected God.
But then, our expectations were met with the mystery of not SEEING what we were expecting. It shifted us.
We didn't mean for it to. It just sort of happened.
We went from EXPECTING, to faithfully believing ABOUT.

That may sound weird to some of you. But that text
message that day—the Father used it to put His
finger on that spot in my heart.

He whispered an invitation to come up, out of that
wilderness, leaning on my Beloved.

I sang my way through that season of deep loss.
Living Room Sessions is the fruit of that. But I lost
my expectation somewhere along the way. And now,
I believe the Father deeply desires to heal and restore
our expectancy, friend. To take the tangled mess of
experience and mystery and meet us right there in
that wilderness.

He doesn't want us to survive on faithfulness.
He wants to restore to us fellowship.
Expectancy is the fruit of fellowship.

The only way out of the wilderness... is leaning on
our beloved (Song of Solomon 8:5).

Prayerful Meditation:
Father, I confess that my heart fainted somewhere in the middle of my ache
and disappointment. I stopped leaning and started going through the motions
of my faith. The mystery was crippling to my heart and to our relationship.

Today, I am asking that you would lead me out of this wilderness. I'm asking
that every wall I've built between us, in self-preservation, would be torn
down. Today, I choose to lean into you again. To trust your frame to sustain
me in my weakness, to support me in my grief. I'm returning to the table.
I want to sit with you again. I want to believe what you say and expect the
evidence of it. Help me, Jesus. I am yours.

NOTES

1. Trotter, Lilias. "Quotes from the writings of Lilias Trotter." *LiliasTrotter.com.* 06 February 1903. https://liliastrotter.com/quotes/

2. Song of Solomon 2:11-13 TPT

3. Psalm 37:25 NIV

4. Lyte, Henry Francis. "Abide With Me! Fast Falls The Even Tide." Hymnary.org. https://hymnary.org/text/abide_with_me_fast_falls_the_eventide

5. Joy, Joyful, Rejoice – Biblegateway.com

6. Romans 7:15 NIV

7. Dickinson, Emily. "The Complete Poems of Emily Dickinson" Goodreads.com https://www.goodreads.com/quotes/284004-to-see-the-summer-sky-is-poetry-though-never-in

8. James 1:11

9. Ephesians 5:26

10. Hebrews 11:1

11. Van Gogh, Vincent. "Vincent van Gogh" *QuoteFancy.com.* n.d. https://quotefancy.com/quote/927869

12. John 12:24

13. Psalm 23

14. 1 Samuel 16:7

15. 1 Corinthians 15:31 NKJV

16. Switchfoot. "The Shadow Proves the Sunshine." Youtube. https://www.youtube.com/watch?v=rTR7pCEZhhI

17. Proverbs 21:12

18. Matthew 12:34

19. John 15:13

20. Luke 11:9

21. John 8:44-45

22. John 4:20

23. Luke 6:27

24. Lucado, Max. "Max Lucado" *dailychristianquote. com*. Katherine Walden. Jan. 5, 2022. https://www. dailychristianquote.com/max-lucado-14/

25. Proverbs 25:13 NASB

26. 1 Corinthians 13:13

27. John 15:5

28. Proverbs 13:12

29. Psalm 27:13 NIV

GRATITUDE

It's difficult to capture in a few words the multitude of radiant hearts to which my deep gratitude for this book is due. I ache that I had the time and space to name each and every one, but please know that I am deeply grateful for you!

- To my Mama, Sherry Lynn, you showed me the beauty of words and taught me that no matter the challenge we're facing, there's a way to conquer it! To the most resourceful and diligent woman I know, thank you for cheering so loudly for me for the last 42 years.

- Pops, from the hours you spent with us curled in your lap while you read from the magical writings of C.S. Lewis and the timeless treasures of scripture, you marked my life with a love for words, for THE Word. Thank you for being the first man in my life to champion my voice.

- To the absolute love of my life and my best friend, Ryan Paul... you have lifted me with your life. You have cheered for me and wept with me. The stories in this book were lived WITH you and there will never be enough words to capture my deep gratitude for you.

- To my beautiful children, Malachai, Aidah, Jedediah, Faith, Titus, Miah, and Fynley... this book is really for you. Thank you for the hours together that you sacrificed so I could write it! Thank you for your sweet encouragement along the way. May you forever dive deep into the holy wonder of God With Us.

- Mom Landis, Ellen Engle, Amy Perkins, Bri Sweatt, Leah Wood, Jordan Middlebrook – Thank you for pouring through these sloppy pages with me in its early stages! For lifting my heart to excellence, your incredible attention to detail, and cheering me on along the way! "In an abundance of counselors there is safety." Proverbs 11:14

- Grahm and Sarah Foster ("friend"). You prayed for me, cheered for me, photographed me, and kept reminding me that this book was in me every time I wanted to quit. I am forever grateful, and I love you deep.

- Nika Maples, my glorious and anointed book coach, You showed me the way of obedience. Thank you for reminding me that I am a tree meant to bear fruit. Thank you for delighting in the fruit with me.

- Alisa Keeton, you opened your home and heart to me and taught me how to embody these words, this worship. It was sustenance through the rigor of writing (which you know well). I love you and am better because of you.

- Shawn Landis, my brother, and friend. You are a creative genius! Thank you for your grace as I fleshed out the visual dream of this book. The beauty you helped me create will be treasured forever.

- Nate and Christy Johnston, you guys are beautiful! Christy, I am honored and humbled by your generous words and so grateful for the way you both cheer for the body of Christ so well. You are true pioneers and we love you.

- To the MANY remarkable friends of God who have prayerfully and financially partnered with us through The Missional Nomads and Ryan and Nina Landis Ministries over the last decade… your faithfulness has kissed our hearts with the kindness of God. Your generosity has made way for His kingdom to advance and been a co-labor even as I've written this book! We are deeply grateful for each one of you!

- Sharon Swaffer and KC Woodward, you do not know each other, but you both planted seeds of hope for this book years before it was a glimmer in my eye. That will never be lost on me! It is the definition of loving well and I am so grateful!

- Lauralee Whitman and Mary Beth Sponsler, no one knows how many of these stories have you both quietly in the background, holding my heart with your love and your friendship. I love you deep my faithful friends. Thank you for loving me.

And finally, to the keeper of my heart, King Jesus. You are my favorite place. You sustain me with your perfect love, and I am eternally and wildly devoted to you. Until every voice declares your worth with me, I will keep singing .

ABOUT THE AUTHOR

Nina Landis is a worshiper, writer, pastor, songwriter, homeschool mom, and sourdough enthusiast. She has written, collaborated on, and recorded over fifteen musical works and has been pastoring and discipling communities for over twenty years. She and her husband, Ryan, after spending ten years traveling as itinerate worship leaders, founded The Missional Nomads in 2020: a ministry committed to encouraging, counseling, and practically serving weary pastors and ministry leaders around the nation.

She has devoted her adult life to strengthening the body of Christ to grow in greater depth and communion with God. She is passionate about the worth and preeminence of Jesus as the primary aim of our lives and is wholehearted in her pursuit of Christ receiving the reward of His suffering through the simple devotion of His bride, the church.

Nina currently lives in the captivating mountains of Colorado and loves the adventure of the outdoors, all things whole-health, and cozying up by the fire with a good book and a cup of tea. She is the proud mother of seven children, four with her and three in heaven, and has been happily married to her remarkable husband Ryan for over twenty years.

Follow Nina's Ministry:
www.RyanandNinaLandis.com
www.TheMissionalNomads.com

Instagram: @ninalandis
Spotify: Nina Landis

9 798218 425623